Printing and the Book
in Fifteenth-Century England
A Bibliographical Survey

Printing and the Book in Fifteenth-Century England

A Bibliographical Survey by
Walter L. Heilbronner

Published for the Bibliographical Society
of the University of Virginia
The University Press of Virginia
Charlottesville

Preface

In 1936 the Wiegendruck-Gesellschaft published, under the general editorship of Erich von Rath, a work entitled *Der Buchdruck des 15. Jahrhunderts, eine bibliographische Übersicht.* This work, still the only bibliography specifically designed to suit the needs of the incunabulist, appeared precisely a century after the death of the immortal Ludwig Hain – in Munich, lonely and impoverished. The volume was issued in an edition of only five hundred numbered copies; today it is rarely found in the antiquarian market and commands a correspondingly high price. The various sections of the *Buchdruck* were compiled over a span of years, beginning in 1929; that devoted to England (pp. 73–84, with a total of 105 entries) was the work of Rudolf Juchhoff. Since that time other bibliographical lists, useful for the incunabulist, have appeared from time to time. *Studies in Bibliography*, for example, annually provides a most comprehensive one of books and articles on early printing published within the year – but these lists are not, of course, cumulative nor could they be arranged by subject, as the student of the earliest books would wish them to be.

In the light of these comments, it is surely quite proper to express the hope that the present volume may prove to be the first of a series of surveys designed to bring the German bibliography up to date. The fine industry of Professor Walter L. Heilbronner has unearthed over four hundred pertinent entries, thus almost quadrupling the 1936 total of studies on English incunables. On the one hand, this points up, numerically in any case, the urgent need for such a revision; on the other, the peruser of this volume will soon perceive, from Professor Heilbronner's annotated list, how much important work has been done in this field, on both sides of the Atlantic, since the publication of the German list.

If the growth of bibliographical studies on non-English incunabula has been proportionately as great, then the need for a new, comprehensive bibliography is perfectly self-evident. Indeed, there is every reason to believe that an even greater amount of research has been expended on Continental incunabula, for there are many more such editions and the copies are more widely distributed. Recently, the Slavic and East European countries have begun to contribute their share of publications to the grand total. The task of ferreting out all the published material will surely be a most exacting one – but it would be splendid, indeed, if the Bibliographical Society of the University of Virginia could sponsor a project so widely useful. Professor Heilbronner's admirable volume provides just the proper impetus for embarking on such an undertaking.

The Pierpont Morgan Library   CURT F. BÜHLER
New York, New York

Contents

Introduction

Old books must be loved, and their idiosyncracies [sic] *carefully studied, before they will yield up all their treasures; that done, the observant lover will obtain possession of both soul and body; he may revel in the intellectual feast provided by the author, or he may study the material and mechanical features of the books as represented by the peculiarities of paper and the habits and customs of the various printers. Then, grouping these as a botanist does his flowers, according to their organisation into classes, orders, genera, and species, he may extract from his volumes true replies to questions which otherwise would remain hidden for ever. So true is the dictum, "The Mind it is which sees, and not the Eye alone."* [1]

These words of the great Caxton biographer William Blades have, in a sense, served as a guideline for this compilation. It is hoped that the listings in this volume, with the index, will facilitate the grouping and organization mentioned by Blades.

When this work was begun some three years ago, it was intended to be nothing more than a continuation of *Der Buchdruck des 15. Jahrhunderts*,[2] whose publication was completed for all countries in 1932. As the project evolved, it was soon discovered that the likely titles listed in various bibliographies could be most misleading. Too many of these works had little or nothing to do with fifteenth-century English printers or printing. Thus, for example, many promising titles proved to be catalogs containing no English incunabula or were general histories of various aspects of printing with either no or only the slightest reference to England at the period under examination. Thus Alfred Pollard's *An Essay on Colophons* (Chicago, 1905) did not include any English colophons. Examples of this sort turned up with depressing frequency. It thus became obvious that a careful examination of the works themselves was necessary. Mere reliance on a plausible title would have brought with it a high incidence of wrong listings.

This extremely time-consuming but essential examination of each work could be reflected in descriptive annotations and commentaries with great advantage to the potential user. It is hoped that such an expansion of the original plan will not only make this work more useful to the bibliographer and incunabulist but will also extend its

[1] William Blades, "Typography and Bibliography," "*The Boke of Saint Albans*," by Dame Juliana Berners (London, 1899), p. 16.
[2] Rudolph Juchhoff, ed., "Der Buchdruck Englands und der nordischen Länder im fünfzehnten Jahrhundert," Part IV of *Der Buchdruck des 15. Jahrhunderts* (Berlin, 1930), pp. 73–84.

scope to other fields. The pertinence of a particular work can be ascertained, though the item is not immediately available to the user. Much of the time, effort, and expense often expended in obtaining books or journals through interlibrary loan or on microfilm can thus be lessened.

The present listing is somewhat more inclusive than either the original German compilation or the "Selective Checklist," an annual compilation in *Studies in Bibliography*. In order to broaden the general applicability of the work, pertinent semitechnical and popular literature dealing with the subject of fifteenth-century English printing and printers is included as well as scholarly works. To cite only two examples, a one-act children's play on Caxton and a teen-age fictional biography of England's first printer are entered. Also works treating only literary and linguistic problems of the period are listed and thus identified if their primary stress is on incunabula.

Although the bibliographer invariably hopes that nothing of importance is omitted, no claim for completeness is made here. Aside from the basis provided by *Der Buchdruck des 15. Jahrhunderts* and by the "Selective Checklist," a large number of book and periodical bibliographies were carefully searched under all possible headings. In addition, cross checks and spot checks were made on the basis of bibliographical entries in carefully and broadly selected monographs, biographies, and journal articles. In a very few instances a periodical or book was available neither in the Library of Congress nor through the Union Catalog. If such a title seemed at all pertinent, it was included in this listing with the notation "Not examined" under the bibliographic entry.

Owing to the specialized nature and the particular emphasis of the present work, it was impossible to follow *The MLA Style Sheet* closely. The main aim was consistency, this being considered more important than following a previously established specific system of notation.

A special problem was posed by lectures which were published one or several years after their initial presentation. Where the year of publication differs from the year in which the lecture was given, the main entry is under the date of publication, with a cross reference under the year of delivery.

Although innumerable reprints and facsimiles of incunabula have been published over the years, these are not usually listed unless they were published with editorial comments or with sufficient pertinent historical, biographical, bibliographical, literary, or linguistic annotation. An even greater selectivity was exercised with regard to general histories of printing. A few of the most popular and useful ones are given.

Catalogs of libraries and collections are listed separately in Part I of the compilation. Only a relatively small number – hopefully the most significant – are actually included. No attempt is made to refer to every catalog that contains English incunabula. The number of catalogs and checklists citing English incunabula is so large that examination prior to inclusion would have protracted the completion of this work without adding greatly to its overall usefulness. The location of English incunabula can be ascertained without too much difficulty in those few countries for which a census has been prepared, namely,

The United States: Goff, Frederick R. *Incunabula in American Libraries. A Third Census* .... New York, 1964.

Belgium: Polain, Louis. *Catalogue des livres imprimés au quinzième siècle des bibliothèques de Belgique.* Brussels, 1932.

France: Pellechet, M. L. C. *Catalogue général des incunables des bibliothèques publiques de France.* Paris, 1897–1909.

The absence of a census for Great Britain, other than the *STC*, is especially serious, but it may be noted that the major holdings of English incunabula in Great Britain are in the British Museum and the John Rylands Library. Various Oxford libraries, especially the Bodleian, and the college libraries of Cambridge have varying numbers of frequently unique or near unique items. J. C. T. Oates's catalog for the Cambridge University Library is listed, but for other colleges it will be necessary to refer to their lists or catalogs.

It also needs to be noted that several works dealing exclusively with sixteenth-century printing are included. As Wynkyn de Worde, Julian Notary, and Richard Pynson lived well into the sixteenth century and were extremely productive then, it was deemed appropriate to go beyond the artificial demarcation of the turn of the century and include several entries concerning these men and their works.

The sequence of the listings is chronological, a method most appriate for this type of work and also used in the earlier German compilation. Thus all main entries, including those in the catalog section, are arranged by year of imprint. Entries are arranged alphabetically by author or editor within any one year. This system, in a few instances, has led to paradox in that one author will comment on another's work with the earlier one appearing later in the listing because of the alphabetical requirements. All such rates are supplied with cross references.

A special problem was posed by the fourth and fifth series of *The Library*. In the fourth series the quarterly issues appeared from mid-year to mid-year, a practice that was continued with the fifth series until 1951. The title page for the annual volume shows the volume number and only one year. Thus the four issues that appeared for 1926–1927 are listed, on the title page, as 1927 only. This practice was also followed for the listings in this work. Beginning with Volume V (1951) of the fifth series, *The Library* was again published on an annual basis. Because of the contraction into one calendar year, Volume VI is also dated 1951. To maintain consistency in the listings the date of publication provided on the title page is used in this compilation. As the volume number is in any case logical, the user should have no difficulty in locating the proper issue.

Because the primary concern, even in the case of text editions, is less with the text than with the editorial apparatus supplied, an edited text is cited under the editor's name rather than under the name of the author of the original work.

The listings in the Index are intended to facilitate the use of the compilation. A specific example will illustrate the method followed. Christine de Pisan's *Book of Fayttes of Armes and of Chyualry*, translated by William Caxton, was published by the Early English Text Society in 1932. The editor for this edition was A. T. P. Byles. The main entry lists the work with Byles as an author entry, though he is identified as the editor. In the Index the work is listed under "Byles, A. T. P.," and "Pisan, Christine de," as well as under other appropriate headings such as "Caxton" as both printer and translator. This somewhat unusual procedure can be justified on the basis of the primary purpose of this compilation.

In the long process of examining and reading the many works cited, rather curious discoveries were made. Thus even a cursory examination of the items treating Caxton's work in its linguistic and literary ramifications will point up the fact that many, if not most, of the articles and monographs dealing with this facet of the first English printer were written by foreigners. Moreover, it was found that a fairly unique manner of celebrating the discovery of a Caxton imprint took place nearly a century ago. F. J. Furnivall tells us that upon finding a copy of the *Book of Curtesye* he "drank seven cups of tea, and ate five or six large slices of bread and butter, in honour of the event."[3] In the age of the dry martini this would scarcely be considered adequate.

Some of the dangers of becoming enamored with one's subject, even if this is as important a figure as Caxton, are evident in the following evaluation made by one of his nineteenth-century American admirers:

He [Caxton] may be called the one great man of England – for he was the leader in the introduction into that country of the mysteri-

[3]Frederick J. Furnivall, *Caxton's "Book of Curtesye"* (Early English Text Society, Extra Series, No. III; London, 1868), p. [v].

ous art that has raised to the commercial and brain supremacy of the globe, an island little larger than the State of Iowa; it was he who put his hand to that mysterious calling no Englishman had touched before him.[4]

For a different perspective on and orientation toward Caxton and printing in general, a citation from the final paragraph of a work entitled *Caxton and the Art of Printing* would seem appropriate. This book was issued during the fifth decade of the nineteenth century by the American Sunday-School Union in the United States and by the Religious Tract Society in England. It states that

its [the Society's] great rule is, that each of its publications shall contain a clear statement of the method of a sinner's recovery from guilt and misery by the atonement and grace of the Redeemer, so that if a person were to read a tract even of the smallest size, and should never have the opportunity of seeing another, he might plainly be taught, that in order to [obtain] salvation he must be born again of the Holy Spirit, and justified by faith in the atonement and finished righteousness of Christ.[5]

In conclusion, I wish to thank the many people who, in so many ways, have made this work possible. Mr. John Cook Wyllie, then Librarian of the Alderman Library of the University of Virginia, first suggested this undertaking to me and, over the long period of its development, made many invaluable suggestions and provided continuous help and encouragement.

I owe a special debt of thanks to Dr. Curt F. Bühler of the Pierpont Morgan Library and to Dr. Rudolf Hirsch of the Library of the University of Pennsylvania, both of whom supported the general idea of this project when I first presented it to them. They also favored the suggestion that this volume should be the first of a series of surveys to bring the various sections of *Der Buchdruck des 15. Jahrhunderts* up to date. Dr. Bühler graciously agreed to write the preface for this volume, and Dr. Hirsch went over the entire manuscript. The latter's valuable critical observations and editorial comments and suggestions were gladly incorporated. It must be added, however, that evaluative comments on the entries and any possible errors or omissions up to 1964 are solely my own responsibility.

However, an unfortunate accident in which my entire library, including all the working papers for this survey, was destroyed, has made it impossible for me to incorporate all the valuable sugges-

---

[4] John Springer, *A Few Preliminary Thoughts Toward an Essay on the Life and Character of William Caxton, the First English Printer* (Iowa City, 1877), p. [3].

[5] *Caxton and the Art of Printing* (London, Philadelphia, [185?]), p. 192.

tions for improvements made by the editors of the Press and to include later material which had already been collected.

The Research Committee of the University of Virginia provided funds for incidental travel expenses and for the procurement of microfilms. The Committee for Research Fellowships in the Humanities awarded me a grant for the summer of 1965, which made possible the completion of the project during this period. I wish to express my gratitude to the members of both committees, especially to their respective chairmen, Professor Julian Bishko and Professor Francis J. Brooke.

Mr. William H. Runge, Curator of Rare Books, Mr. N. Harvey Deal, then Reference Librarian, and the late Miss Louise Savage, Acquisitions Librarian, all of the Alderman Library, contributed greatly to this work by making available the facilities of their departments. To them also I wish to express my thanks.

To the members of the Publications Committee of the Bibliographical Society of the University of Virginia I am indebted for their acceptance of this work for publication under the Society's auspices.

During many late evenings my wife helped read proof on the main entries, a painstaking and dreary task which goes beyond the normal demands of marital duties, and one which deserves acknowledgment. Last but not least, I must thank my son David, who assisted me in reading and correcting the typed manuscript of the index, and did this without requesting the monetary or other tribute usually desired by teenagers.

WALTER L. HEILBRONNER

Cortland, New York
September, 1966

Part I

Catalogs and Checklists

BULLEN, GEORGE and ECCLES, GREGORY W. *Catalogue of the Books in the Library of the British Museum Printed in England, Scotland and Ireland, and of the Books in English Printed Abroad to the Year 1640.* 3 vols. London, 1848.   1

   The catalog is arranged alphabetically by author.
   Index of subjects, with class headings, in Vol. III (pp. 1647–1734).
   "Index of Printers, Booksellers, and Stationers" in Vol. III (pp. 1735–1787).

BLADES, WILLIAM. *A Catalogue of Books Printed by (or Ascribed to the Press of) William Caxton; in Which Is Included the Press-Mark of Every Copy Contained in the Library of the British Museum.* London, 1865. 38 pp.   2

   For description see entry No. 62.

PROCTOR, ROBERT. Part I, Section III of *An Index to the Early Printed Books in the British Museum: From the Invention of Printing to the Year MD. With Notes of Those in the Bodleian Library.* London, 1898.   3

   A listing, not complete, of the incunabula in the British Museum. Arranged by country, place of imprint, and printer. Listed chronologically under printer.
   Pertinent are: Bruges (p. 682); Westminster (pp. 714–719); Oxford (pp. 719–720); London (pp. 720–724); St. Albans (p. 724).
   Also later printings of 1930 and 1960.

SAYLE, CHARLES E. *Early English Printed Books in the University Library, Cambridge (1475-1640).* 4 vols. Cambridge [Eng.], 1900-1907.   4

   Lists holdings. Only Vol. I is directly pertinent here. Each entry is briefly described. The listings are arranged by place of publication and by printer.
   "Westminster" (pp. 1–15): Caxton (41 items); Wynkyn de Worde (21 items); Julian Notary (1 item); Barbier (1 item).
   "Oxford" (pp. 11–17): 1478 (2 items); Rood (7 items); Rood and Hunte (1 item).
   "St. Albans" (pp. 18–19): "Schoolmaster Printer" (6 items).
   "London" (pp. 19–24): Lettou (2 items); Lettou and Machlinia (5 items); Machlinia (10 items); Pynson (11 items).
   "Bruges" (p. 26): Caxton (2 items).
   Volume IV contains indexes of printers, towns, books, and the like.
   Now largely superseded by J. C. T. Oates (see No. 25).

BURGER, KONRAD. *The Printers and Publishers of the XVth Century with Lists of Their Works; Index to the "Supplement" to Hain's "Repertorium bibliographicum."* London, 1902 (reprinted Berlin, 1926; Milan, 1950).   5
Includes English printers and their products together with bibliographical references.

HAEBLER, KONRAD. "England," in Abt. II of *Typenrepertorium der Wiegendrucke.* Leipzig, 1905. pp. [355]-360, and *ibid.*, V (1924), 167.   6
A basic work for the bibliographer and incunabulist. Provides descriptions as well as other pertinent data on type used during the incunabula period. Essentially follows the numbering system established by Proctor.
A new edition, with revisions, is in preparation.

J. PIERPONT MORGAN LIBRARY. *Early Printed Books; France (End), The Netherlands, Spain and England.* Vol. III, *Catalogue of Manuscripts and Early Printed Books from the Libraries of William Morris, Richard Bennett, Bertram, Fourth Earl of Ashburnham, and Other Sources. Now Forming Portion of the Library of J. Pierpont Morgan.* London, 1906-1907.   7
English incunabula on pp. 163-237. Lists and describes in detail, with facsimiles. Includes books printed by Caxton, Lettou, Machlinia, Wynkyn de Worde, Pynson, and Notary. Also Oxford and St. Albans imprints.

GESELLSCHAFT FÜR TYPENKUNDE. *Veröffentlichungen.* Halle [later Leipzig], 1907-1939.   8
Plates illustrate type pages and individual letters of English incunabula. 1630 – Richard Pynson; 1790 – Machlinia, Type 4; 1791 – Machlinia, Type 5; 1792 – Wynkyn de Worde, Type 3; 1793 – Wynkyn de Worde, Type [3]5; 2150 – Caxton, Type 6; 2274 – "Possibly English"; 2275 – Caxton, Type 2*; 2460 – Not available for examination.

DE RICCI, SEYMOUR. *A Census of Caxtons.* Oxford, 1909. 196 pp. (Bibliographical Society. Illustrated Monographs, 15.)   9
Classifies works from Caxton's press in the same order as does Duff (see No. 154). For details see entry No. 170.

DUFF, EDWARD GORDON. *Fifteenth Century English Books. A Bibliography of Books and Documents Printed in England and of Books for the English Market Printed Abroad.* Oxford, 1917. lx, 123 pp. (Bibliographical Society. Illustrated Monographs, No. 18.)   10
A complete listing, as known at the time, of all extant copies of 15th-century English books. Has 431 entries with detailed descriptions of the different imprints, noting variations where pertinent. Also provides lo-

cation of copies. This work is based on collations and close examination
of the books.

"List of Facsimiles" (pp. 121–123).

"Typographical Index" (pp. 125–136).

Attention is drawn to the section "Books ... Printed Abroad," listed
carefully by Duff but unfortunately without bibliographical references to
the standard bibliographies of incunabula, e.g. M. F. A. G. Campbell, *Annales de la typographie néerlandaise* (The Hague, 1874–1890).

COLE, GEORGE WATSON.   *Check-List or Brief Catalogue of
the Library of Henry Huntington* [*English Literature to 1640*]. New
York, 1919.   11

Also supplement: *Check-List or Brief Catalogue of the English
Books, 1475–1640, in the Henry E. Huntington Library and Art Gallery.* New York, 1920. (Additions and Corrections, July 1919-June
1920.)

Lists holdings of English books for the dates indicated.

Superseded by Mead (see No. 19) for 15th-century imprints.

WINSHIP, GEORGE P.   *Census of Fifteenth Century Books Owned
in America; Compiled by a Committee of the Bibliographical Society
of America.* New York, 1919.   12

A general listing including English incunabula. Contains no index, but
some cross references. Alphabetically arranged by author. Lists printers
only if they edited or translated. Lack of a proper index is a major defect
in the work and greatly restricts its usefulness.

Superseded by Stillwell's *Second Census* (No. 22) and Goff's *Third
Census* (No. 31).

STEARNS, MAE I.   *Check List of Books Printed in English Before 1641.* Chicago, 1923.   13

Lists holdings of the Newberry Library. Arranged alphabetically by author with "Index of Printers, Booksellers and Stationers" (pp. 187–198).
For 15th-century imprints superseded by Butler (No. 18).

HASKELL, DANIEL C.   "Check-List of Early English Printing,
1475–1640, in the New York Public Library." *New York Public Library. Bulletin,* 29 (1925), 484–512, 545–578.   14

Entries are arranged alphabetically by author. Lacks index.

POLLARD, ALFRED W. and REDGRAVE, G. R.   *A Short-Title
Catalogue of Books Printed in England, Scotland and Ireland and of
English Books Printed Abroad, 1475–1640.* London, 1926 (reprinted
1946).   15

Supersedes and expands the *Catalogue* edited by Bullen and Eccles
(1884). The present work is a bibliography of known copies. Only copies
not in the British Museum are located.

See also: Morrison, P. G. *Index of Printers, Publishers, and Book-sellers* (No. 24).

A new edition, with revisions by the late William Jackson, is to be published soon.

JUCHHOFF, RUDOLF, ed.   "Der Buchdruck Englands und der nordischen Länder im fünfzehnten Jahrhundert," Part IV of *Der Buchdruck des 15. Jahrhunderts; eine bibliographische Übersicht.* Berlin, 1930. pp. 73–84.   16
A listing of works dealing with 15th-century printing in England. No descriptive or critical commentary. Listings are in chronological sequence, with the last entry dated 1929.

GUPPY, HENRY.   *English Incunabula in the John Rylands Library. A Catalogue of Books Printed in England and of English Books Printed Abroad Between the Years 1475 and 1500. With Chronological Index, Index of Printers and Stationers, Subject Index and Sixteen Facsimiles.* Manchester, 1931.   17
"Author Catalogue" (pp. 1–81). Books listed alphabetically by author and described.
"Chronological Index" (pp. 83–89).
"Index of Printers and Booksellers" (pp. 90–97).
"Subject Index" (pp. 98–102).

BUTLER, PIERCE.   *A Check List of Fifteenth Century Books in the Newberry Library and in Other Libraries in Chicago.* Chicago, 1933.   18
Supersedes the earlier editions of 1919 and 1923. Lists 1,613 incunabula then in the Newberry Library and 182 found in other Chicago libraries. Has concordance of Hain numbers, an index of authors, titles, and printers, and an index of cities.

MEAD, HERMAN RALPH.   *Incunabula in the Huntington Library.* San Marino, Cal., 1937. (Huntington Library Lists, No. 3.)   19
Arranged by country and place of printing. Follows Proctor's *Index.* Items 5217 to 5283 are English incunabula.

THURSTON, ADA and BÜHLER, CURT F.   *Check List of Fifteenth Century Printing in the Pierpont Morgan Library.* New York, 1939.   20
A listing of the holdings. "England" (pp. 166–174). Caxton is also listed under Bruges (p. 157).

WOODWARD, GERTRUDE L.   *English Books and Books Printed in England Before 1641 in the Newberry Library. A Supplement to the Record in the "Short Title Catalogue."* Chicago, 1939.   21
Lists titles and new purchases. No index.

STILLWELL, MARGARET B. *Incunabula in American Libraries. A Second Census of Fifteenth Century Books Owned in the United States, Mexico, and Canada.* New York, 1940. (Bibliographical Society of America. Monograph Series, No. 1.) 22
   Supersedes Winship's *Census of Fifteenth Century Books Owned in America* (New York, 1919).
   Uses Hain for author entries; when author unknown follows *BMC* or *Gesamtkatalog*. An invaluable work for locating incunabula.
   "List of Registered Owners" (pp. xv–xxxv).
   "List of Abbreviations" (pp. xxxvii–xlv).
   "Incunabula in American Libraries" (pp. 1–525).
   "Variant Author Forms and Entries" (pp. 527–542).
   "Concordances" (pp. 543–610).
   Superseded by Goff's *Incunabula in American Libraries* (No. 31).

BISHOP, WILLIAM WARNER. *A Checklist of American Copies of "Short-Title Catalogue" Books.* 2nd ed., Ann Arbor, 1950. 23
   Lists *STC* numbers in sequence with location in American libraries indicated by symbols. The second edition has a supplement of additions to the *STC*.
   First published in 1944.

MORRISON, PAUL G. *Index of Printers, Publishers and Booksellers in A. W. Pollard and G. R. Redgrave: A Short-Title Catalogue of Books Printed in England, Scotland and Ireland and of English Books Printed Abroad, 1475–1640.* Charlottesville, 1950 (reprinted 1961). 24
   The index is alphabetically arranged. Provides the *STC* numbers for each printer, publisher, and bookseller. An extremely useful index which widens the scope of the *STC*.
   The second printing has "a few corrections."

OATES, JOHN C. T. *A Catalogue of the Fifteenth-Century Printed Books in the University Library, Cambridge.* Cambridge [Eng.], 1954. 25
   The catalogue is divided by countries and the latter by cities of imprint.
   Bruges (pp. 635–636): Caxton, 1st press; items 3306–3308.
   Westminster (pp. 671–686): Caxton, 2nd press; items 4059–4114; Wynkyn de Worde; items 4115–4156; Notary, 2nd press; items 4157 and 4158.
   Oxford (pp. 686–688): Printer of *Expositio S. Hieronymi*; items 4159 and 4160; Theodoric Rood; items 4161–4172.
   London (pp. 688–693): John Lettou, items 4173 and 4174; Lettou and Machlinia; items 4175–4182; Machlinia; items 4183–4193; Pynson; items 4194–4207; Notary, 1st press, with J. Barbier and I. H.; item 4208.
   St. Albans (pp. 693–694): The Schoolmaster Printer; items 4209–4215.
   Index of "Authors and Anonymous Titles" (pp. 701–794).
   Index of "Printers and Places" (pp. 795–817).

Index of "Provenances" (pp. 818–864).
Concordances (pp. 865–889).

O'DELL, STERG. "A Chronological List of Prose Fiction Printed
in England and Other Countries, 1475–1640." Cambridge, Mass.,
1954. (Reproduced from typed manuscript.)   26
    A brief introduction (pp. 1–22) discusses literary aspects, but does not
include commentary on printing. Works are listed chronologically with no-
tations of location of original copies. Fifteenth-century imprints listed
(pp. 23–26), with 16th-century imprints of Wynkyn de Worde and Pynson
noted under appropriate dates.
    The work is useful, though restricted in scope.

RINGLER, WILLIAM. "A Bibliographical and First-Line Index of
English Verse Printed Through 1500; a Supplement to Brown and
Robbins' *Index of Middle English Verse.*" *Bibliographical Society
of America. Papers,* 49 (1955), 153–180.   27
    Brief introduction (pp. 153–156) outlines the rationale of the index.
    "Fifteenth-Century Books Containing English Verse" (pp. 157–160).
This section is arranged according to *STC* numbers. Each entry lists author, title, translator if any, printer, imprint date, total number, and index
numbers of poems included, as well as location and identifying number of
copy used.
    "Probably Printed After 1500" (pp. 160–161). Follows pattern used in
15th-century listings.

RAMAGE, DAVID. *A Finding-List of English Books to 1640 in Libraries in the British Isles. (Excluding the National Libraries and
the Libraries of Oxford and Cambridge).* Durham [Eng.], 1958.   28
    Lists *STC* numbers with symbols indicating the libraries where the
works are located. Supplement lists titles and locations of books not
listed in the *STC.*

COOK, OLAN V. *Incunabula in the Hanes Collection of the Library of the University of North Carolina.* Enlarged ed., Chapel
Hill, 1960.   29
    Lists 4 works printed by Caxton, 2 by Wynkyn de Worde, 1 by Machlinia,
and 3 unassigned (pp. 96–97).

WILLIAMS, FRANKLIN B. *Index of Dedications and Commendatory
Verses in English Books Before 1641.* London, 1962.   30
    Uses serial numbers of the *STC.* For effective use of this work it is
essential that pp. [xx]–xxi be read.
    "Personal Index" (pp. [1]–206).
    "Institutional and Geographical" index (pp. [207]–226).
    "Anonymous and Bibliographical" index (pp. [227]–256).
    Includes only books printed in England except for those books printed

abroad that are in English, Welsh, or Gaelic. This is a most useful work for the literary scholar and bibliographer.

GOFF, FREDERICK R. *Incunabula in American Libraries. A Third Census of Fifteenth-Century Books Recorded in North American Collections.* New York, 1964. 31

Closely follows the pattern of Stillwell's *Second Census* (No. 22), which it supersedes.

"Register of Owners" (pp. [xxiii]–li).

"Incunabula in American Libraries" (pp. [3]–638).

"Variant Author-Forms and Entries" (pp. [637]–655).

"Index of Printers and Publishers" (pp. [657]–714).

Concordances (pp. [715]–789).

Part II

Survey of Works Dealing with
Fifteenth-Century English Printing

ATKYNS, RICHARD. *The Original and Growth of Printing: Collected out of History, and the Records of This Kingdome. Wherein Is Also Demonstrated that Printing Appertaineth to the Prerogative Royal; and Is a Flower of the Crown of England.* London, 1664. 24 pp.   32

Contains much erroneous information, e.g. claims that Gutenberg invented printing in Haarlem, Holland, and that Thomas Bourthier, Archbishop of Canterbury, "moved to their King (Henry the 6th) to use all possible means for procuring a Printing Mold (for so 'twas there called) to be brought into this Kingdom." Links Caxton with Robert Turnour (*sic*); as the latter's subordinate, he was to obtain a press secretly. Makes a detective and industrial espionage story of the introduction of printing into England.

The first press outside of Haarlem and Mainz was established at Oxford, according to Atkyns. The work is today of antiquarian interest only.

MOXON, JOSEPH. *Mechanick Exercises.* London, 1683.   33

The edition of this work by Theodore L. De Vinne in 1896 is now rare and has been superseded by the London 1958 edition by Herbert Davis and Harry Carter. In the latter printing, Moxon's historical sketch of the introduction of printing into England is on pp. 9–10. It follows Atkyns on the Archbishop Bourthier theory.

PALMER, SAMUEL. *The General History of Printing, from Its First Invention in the City of Mentz, to Its First Progress and Propogation thro' the Most Celebrated Cities in Europe. Particularly, Its Introduction, Rise, and Progress Here in England. The Character of the Most Celebrated Printers, from the First Inventors of the Art to the Years 1520 and 1550. With an Account of Their Works.* London, 1732. 400 pp.   34

This is the first comprehensive history of printing in English. Book III, "Of English Printing and Printers" (pp. 313–389) is specifically pertinent. Follows Atkyns in stating that Caxton and Turner were employed to bring Continental printers to England. The individual printers are covered separately.

PALMER, SAMUEL. *A General History of Printing.* London, 1733. 400 pp.   35

This is a reissue of the first edition of 1732 under a slightly different title.

CORSELLIS, F. "On the Alleged Introduction of Printing into England." *Weekly Miscellany*, 26 (April 1735).   36

Not examined.

MIDDLETON, CONYERS.   *A Dissertation Concerning the Origin of Printing in England. Shewing that It Was First Introduced and Practiced by Our Countryman William Caxton, at Westminster; and Not, as Is Commonly Believed, by a Foreign Printer at Oxford.* Cambridge [Eng.], 1735 (2nd ed. 1775). 29 pp.   37
     Discusses the discovery of the Oxford Book of "1468" and rejects the idea that this was the first book printed in England. Also discredits Atkyn's story about Archbishop Bourthier's part in the introduction of printing into England.

LEWIS, JOHN.   *The Life of Mayster Wyllyam Caxton, of the Weald of Kent; The First Printer in England. In Which Is Given an Account of the Rise and Progress of the Art of Pryntyng in England, during This Time, till 1493.* London, 1737. 156 pp.   38
     Stresses Caxton's contribution. Contains much speculation and a number of inaccurate assumptions. It is a highly laudatory and historically interesting work, although not accurate in many details.

AMES, JOSEPH.   *Typographical Antiquities; Being an Historical Account of Printing in England; With Some Memoirs of Our Ancient Printers, and a Register of the Books Printed by Them from the Year MCCCCLXXI to the Year MDC. With an Appendix Concerning Printing in Scotland and Ireland to the Same Time.* London, 1749. 508 pp.   39
     Listings of the then known copies of the books printed by the following printers: Caxton (pp. 1–73); Lettou and Machlinia (pp. 76–78); Wynkyn de Worde (pp. 79–110); Pynson (pp. 111–131). Each entry contains a detailed description of the work itself and includes extensive citations. Illustrations and reproductions of types, watermarks, and initials are included.
     "Of Printing at Oxford" (pp. 437–440) deals with the 15th century. Places the Oxford Book in the year 1478 following the theory expressed by Lewis and Middleton.
     "Of Printing at St. Albans" (pp. 463–466).
     "The General History of Printing in England." Only pp. 484–485 deal with the 15th century.
     The work is obviously dated, but still of interest.

MIDDLETON, CONYERS.   *Dissertation sur l'origine de l'imprimerie en Angleterre.* Trans. by D. G. Imbert. London, 1775.   40
     French translation of the work which first appeared in 1735 (see No. 37).

BOWYER, WILLIAM.   "The Substance of Dr. Middleton's Dissertation on the Origin of Printing in England." Part I of *The Origin of Printing in Two Essays: with Occasional Remarks and an Appendix.* (2nd ed., "with Improvements") London, 1776.   41
     Reprints Middleton's *Dissertation* (No. 37) with disputatious and "correcting" footnotes. Bowyer upholds Atkyn's theory but allows the possi-

bility that Caxton introduced fusil type. The footnotes provide most en-
tertaining examples of 18th-century scholarly insults.

KIPPIS, ANDREW. "Caxton (William)." *Biographia Britannica:
or, the Lives of the Most Emminent Persons Who Have Flourished
in Great Britain and Ireland.* Vol. III. London, 1784.
pp. 351–380. 42
   A general and detailed biography reflecting the knowledge of Caxton at
that time. The author believes that Caxton began printing the *Recuyell* in
Ghent, finished it at Cologne, and then returned to Bruges.
   The notes take up more space than the text. An interesting period piece
of 18th-century biographical scholarship.

AMES, JOSEPH. *Typographical Antiquities: . . . 2nd edition. . . .
Begun by the Late Joseph Ames. Considerably Augmented, Both in
the Memoir and in the Number of Books, by William Herbert, of
Chesthunt, Herts.* 3 vols. London, 1785–1790. 43
   The coverage of the 15th century is essentially the same as in the first
edition (see No. 39).

[AMES, JOSEPH.] *A Catalogue of English Printers; from the Year
1471 to 1600; Most of Them at London.* London, [17—?]. 44
   An alphabetical listing consisting of four pages. Within each letter
heading the arrangement is chronological by date of first printing activity.
   Although no imprint date is given, this little work probably appeared before *Typographical Antiquities* (1749), as on p. 4 there is the following re-
quest: "As the History and Progress of Printing in England, from the year
1474 to the year 1600, is in good forwardness for the Press; if any Gentle-
man please to send the Publisher, Jos. Ames in Wappin, some Account of
these Printers, or add others to them, or oblige him with what may be useful in this Undertaking, the favour will be gratefully acknowledged."

[HASLEWOOD, JOSEPH], ed. *Literary Researches into the History of the "Book of Saint Albans."* London, 1810. 45
   Contains a detailed and scholarly examination of biographical data on
the supposed author, Dame Juliana Berners (pp. 5–20).
   "Biographical Notices" (pp. 21–104) examines, in well-documented detail, the several treatises on the work, the subjects discussed, and the
various editions of the work. This section is amply illustrated with facsimiles of illustrations, type samples, and the like. It is primarily concerned with the 1496 printing by Wynkyn de Worde. The remainder of the
volume is devoted to an excellent facsimile reproduction of this printing.
   The title is also listed as follows: "*Book of St. Albans" Containing
the Treatise of Hawking, Hunting, Coat-Armour, Fishing, and Blasing of
Arms. As Printed at Westminster, by Wynkyn de Worde, the Year of the In-
carnation of Our Lord, 1496. Facsimile Reprint, with Literary Researches
into the History of the Book.*

SINGER, SAMUEL WELLER.   *Some Account of the Book Printed at Oxford in 1468, under the Title of "Exposicio Sancti Jeronimi in Simbolo Apostolorum." In Which Is Examined Its Claim to Be Considered the First Book Printed in England.* London, 1812. 44 pp.   46

   Rejects the contention of Bowyer (see No. 41) that the Oxford Book was printed with wooden type. States that the Oxford Book was "printed by a foreigner at Oxford, who was afterwards interrupted in his typographical labours."

JOHNSON, JOHN.   *Typographia; or, The Printer's Instructor; Including an Account of the Origin of Printing; with Biographical Notices of the Printers of England, from Caxton to the Close of the Sixteenth Century: A Series of Ancient and Modern Alphabets and Domesday Characters, Together with an Elucidation of Every Subject Connected with the Art.* 2 vols. London, 1824.   47

   Only Vol. I is pertinent to this listing.
   The author rejects the theory expressed by Atkyns that the Oxford Book is the first book printed in England; he gives this distinction to one of Caxton's books. This is an interesting, well-documented volume, using and citing earlier scholarship and primary sources. It is, of course, dated and does not reflect many of the more recent discoveries, but it is a fascinating example of thorough and objective research in the early 19th century. Includes detailed descriptions of the incunabula then known.

[STEVENSON, WILLIAM].   *Life of William Caxton, with an Account of the Invention of Printing and of the Modes and Materials Used for Transmitting Knowledge Before That Took Place.* London, 1828. 32 pp. (Published under the Supervision of the Society for the Diffusion of Useful Knowledge; also published as part of *Lives of Eminent Persons* [London, 1833].)   48

   Less a biography than a philosophizing and moralizing account of the history of the art of written communication, going back to antiquity and including digressions on papermaking and the like. Interesting as a period piece.

VAN PRAET, JOSEPH B. B.   *Notice sur Colard Mansion, libraire et imprimeur de la ville de Bruges en Flandre dans le quinzième siècle.* Paris, 1829. 130 pp.   49

   A very brief discussion of Mansion followed by copious notes reflecting also Caxton's association with Mansion. States that Mansion's was the only press in Bruges during the 15th century.

DISRAELI, ISAAC.   *The Amenities of Literature.* London, 1841.   50

   Three essays from this work, all pertaining to printing, were published separately under the title *A Trilogy on Printing History* (No. 302). For description see under latter entry.

KNIGHT, CHARLES. *William Caxton, the First English Printer: A Biography.* London, 1844 (reprinted 1877). 240 pp.   51
   Delves into the history of the book and of England, its customs and mores. Reflects the scholarship and information of his time. Based mainly on Ames's *Typographical Antiquities* (No. 39). Asserts that *De proprietatibus rerum* was printed by Caxton at Cologne.
   Though inaccuracies and unsubstantiated suppositions abound, this is an enjoyable work to read because the author has a rare elegance of style.

LE ROUX DE LINCY, A. J. V. "La vie et les ouvrages de W. Caxton, premier imprimeur anglais." *Revue britannique,* 5e sér., 20 (1844), 78–124.   52
   Asserts that Caxton learned printing in 1468 and that he printed at the Abbey at Westminster. Also that Caxton had brought his presses from Cologne. Claims that Caxton had been acquainted with Gutenberg, Fust, Schoeffer, Mansion, and Zell. Supposes the last-named to have been Caxton's teacher.
   This is a detailed, highly speculative study, obviously filled with errors and assumptions. It is primarily of interest as an early example of Caxton scholarship. The author discusses typographical and other technical details also. A list of then known Caxton books is appended.

JONES, JOHN WINTER. *Observations upon the Discovery of Two Rare Tracts in the Library of the British Museum, Hitherto Unknown, from the Press of William Caxton. Communicated to the Society of Antiquaries in a Letter to Sir Henry Ellis.* London, 1846. Reprinted from: *Archaeologia,* 31 (1846), 412–424.   53
   Compares a copy of *Meditations sur les sept psaulmes penitenciaulx* and a French version of the *Cordiale, sive de quatur novissimis* with known Caxtons. Concludes that these two were printed abroad prior to Caxton's becoming established at Westminster.

RIMBAULT, E. F., *et al.* "Caxton's Printing Office." *Notes and Queries,* 2 (1850), 99, 122, 142, 187, 233, 340.   54
   A series of brief notes by various contributors regarding the location of Caxton's shop at Westminster. The first entry, by E. F. Rimbault, rejects Dibdin's contention that it was actually in the Abbey. He locates the shop in the Almonry, thus still within the precincts of the Abbey. He receives support for this supposition from J. G. Nichols (p. 123). On p. 142 he supposes that Caxton's patron at Westminster was John Esteney, who was abbot from 1475 to 1498.
   An anonymous entry (p. 148) casts aspersions on Nichols for contradicting Stow. "Anonymous" feels that "useful works, which . . . are published at a price that ensures them a circulation of almost unlimited extent"

should be handled reverently. The controversy continues in the subsequent entries.

The last entry (p. 340), by John Cropp, contends that the printing office was indeed in the Abbey chapels, "but in an upper story, a beautiful screen separating the workplace from the most sacred part of the building."

Neither the brevity of these notes nor their fanciful nature justify the extensiveness of this notation, but their occasional bits of amusing personal invective make them more than usually interesting.

Caxton and the Art of Printing.   London, Philadelphia, [185?].
192 pp.   55

This anonymous work was published in the U.S. by the American Sunday School Union and in England by the Religious Tract Society. It is, perhaps, astonishing to see such a title issued by such publishers, but their statement of purpose certainly can be applied not only to Caxton's life but also to many of the books published by him. The publishers of this work desire that all books and tracts issued by them shall be of general utility and of "sound moral tendency."

Only Chapters II and III deal with Caxton; Chapter IV takes up Wynkyn de Worde. Biographical data are of the sketchiest for both printers, the main stress of the author being on homilies suggested by the titles printed by Caxton. These also provide the stimulus for discussion of the nature of sin, death, and other similar topics. The book shows no date of imprint, but because of internal evidence and lack of reference to Blades's work, it was probably published in the sixth decade of the last century.

KNIGHT, CHARLES.   *The Old Printer and the Modern Press.*
London, 1854. 314 pp.   56

Part I, "The Old Printer," is a revised edition of the same author's *William Caxton* (No. 51).

BLADES, WILLIAM, ed.   *The Gouernayle of Helthe: With the Mede-cyne of ye Stomacke. Reprinted from Caxton's Edition, (circa MCCCCXCI). With Introductory Remarks and Notes.* London, 1858.
110 pp.   57

Not examined.

BLADES, WILLIAM, ed.   *Morale Prouerbes, Composed in French by Christyne de Pisan; Translated by the Earl Rivers and Reprinted from the Original Edition of William Caxton, A.D. 1478.* London, 1859. 6 pp.   58

The brief introduction deals primarily with the literary and historical aspects of the work. A short paragraph describes the then known copies of this work.

BLADES, WILLIAM.   "Some Account of the Typography at St. Albans in the 15th Century." [Privately printed], 1860.   59

This work is listed in Blades's *The Pentateuch of Printing* (No. 110) with the following notation: "This went no further than half-a-dozen proofs. — W.B."

FIGGINS, VINCENT, ed. *The Game of Chesse, by William Caxton. Reproduced in Facsimile from a Copy in the British Museum. With a Few Remarks on Caxton's Typographical Productions.* London, 1860. 165 pp. 60

A fine reproduction of text and woodcuts. The edition reproduced here is the second and, according to Figgins, the first work to come from Caxton's press at Westminster. The author believes that Caxton used type cast of pewter and bases his opinion on the appearance of letters. He also provides quite a detailed discussion and comparison of various letters and of the paper used.

BLADES, WILLIAM. *The Life and Typography of William Caxton, England's First Printer. With Evidence of His Typographical Connection with Colard Mansion, the Printer at Bruges. Compiled from Original Sources.* 2 vols. London, 1861–1863. 61

A classic in the field of bibliography and particularly in Caxton studies. Illustrated and heavily documented with original and translated official documents. Proposes that Caxton learned printing from Mansion at Bruges. Rejects the theory that Caxton was first exposed to the art in Cologne. Contains detailed descriptions and discussions of works printed, written, and translated by Caxton.

Much of the distinction of these volumes as a bibliographical and typographical work is due to the anonymous assistance of the eccentric Henry Bradshaw. (See G. W. Prothero, *A Memoir of Henry Bradshaw* [London, 1888], pp. 75–76.)

See also condensations of 1877 (No. 74) and 1882 (No. 92).

BLADES, WILLIAM. *A Catalogue of Books Printed by (or Ascribed to the Press of) William Caxton; in Which Is Included the Press-Mark of Every Copy Contained in the Library of the British Museum.* London, 1865. 38 pp. 62

A handlist of the books in the British Museum printed by Caxton and a catalog of everything produced by Caxton's press. The title of each work is given in full, followed by the pressmark. Other locations are listed if the work is not in the British Museum.

BERJEAU, J. PH. *Early Dutch, German and English Printers' Marks.* London, 1866–[1869]. 100 facsim. 63

The following 15th-century printers are listed (the number after each name refers to the illustration): Julian Notary (23), Wynkyn de Worde (46), St. Albans (54), William Caxton (20).

FURNIVALL, FREDERICK J., ed. *Caxton's "Book of Curtesye;"*
Printed at Westminster About 1477-8 A.D. and Now Reprinted, With
Two MS. Copies of the Same Treatise, From the Oriel MS. 79, and
the Balliol MS. 354. London, 1868. (Early English Text Society.
Extra Series, No. 3.) xii, 57 pp.   64
   A brief but exuberant preface by the editor who "drank seven cups of
tea, and ate five or six large slices of bread and butter, in honour of the
event," the latter being his discovery of the Caxton book here reprinted.
   Derives his basic information on the Caxton printing from Skeat and
Blades. The Caxton text is printed facing the text of Oriel MS. 79.

RAE, JOHN, ed. *The Statutes of Henry VII. In Exact Facsimile,*
from the Very Rare Original, Printed by Caxton in 1489. Edited,
with Notes and Introduction. London, 1869. xxi, 32 pp.   65
   Facsimiles of the statutes enacted by the first three Parliaments of
Henry VII. The introduction (pp. i–xxi) briefly discusses and describes
the extant copies of this Caxton imprint, of which the best is here reproduced. The rest is devoted primarily to a short history of the reign of
Henry VII and the statutes' relationship to their period.

BLADES, WILLIAM. *How to Tell a Caxton; With Some Hints Where*
and How the Same May Be Found. London, 1870. 55 pp.   66
   A little work written to aid the "educated layman" in discovering and
identifying Caxton imprints. With plates and bibliography of Caxtoniana
discovered by that time.

DE VINNE, THEODORE L. "William Caxton," *Printers' Circular,*
7 (Sept., Oct., Nov., Dec., 1872), 241–243, 281–283, 321–323,
353–355.   67
   A worshipful, brief biography in four parts written by a printer who
credits Coster rather than Gutenberg with the invention of the art. Contains many factual errors and also omits much information on Caxton that
was known at the time. Obviously did not know Blades's monumental work
on Caxton, the earliest edition of which was published ten years previously. Curiously enough, however, De Vinne does have an appreciation of
Caxton's great contribution to the English language and to English letters
and culture generally.

MADDEN, JOHN PATRICK AUGUSTE. *Lettres d'un bibliophile,*
2e série, lettre 7: *William Caxton a-t-il imprimé le De proprietati-*
bus rerum? Paris, 1873.   68
   Advances the theory that Caxton learned to print at the Convent of
Weidenbach near Cologne, a theory refuted by Crotch in *The Prologues and*
Epilogues of William Caxton (No. 221), pp. lxxxvii–lxxxviii.

BLADES, WILLIAM. "*Missale ad usum Sarum* and William Caxton." *The Athenaeum* (London), No. 2421 (1874), 392.   69

A brief note announces the discovery of the book printed in Paris for Caxton by Guilerme Maynyal in 1487. Duff lists this as No. 247.

KÖNNECKE, G. *Ein unbekannter Druck von William Caxton aus dem Jahre 1483. In der Bibliotheca Hechto-Heineana zu Halberstadt aufgefunden.* Marburg, 1874. 14 pp. 70

An extremely detailed description of the work, including the paper. The book is complete and consists of 48 pages. The type is described as Caxton's type 4*. The work bears neither title nor date of imprint. It contains six letters exchanged between Pope Sixtus IV and others. The author establishes the date of imprint as 1483 on the basis of a detailed examination of types used by Caxton, utilizing primarily Blades's facsimiles of Caxton types. It is unfortunate that the text is not reprinted together with the description and analysis. The printing is Duff, No. 371, with the title *Sex epistolae.*

MADDEN, JOHN PATRICK AUGUSTE. *Lettres d'un bibliographe,* 4e série, p. 31: *Caxton à Westminster.* Paris, 1875. 71

Disagrees with Blades on several points, but presents no logical alternatives of his own. Ends with a song of praise for Caxton.

MADDEN, JOHN PATRICK AUGUSTE. *Lettres d'un bibliographe,* 4e série, p. 13: *William Caxton.* Paris, 1875. 72

Claims to find French influences in Caxton's type designs, possibly Jenson's, i.e. actually Venetian. Considers Caxton's *Recuyell* to be the first book printed in the English language, but to have been done in Cologne. Makes frequent insulting references to Blades and other scholars.

BLADES, ROWLAND HILL. *Who Was Caxton? William Caxton, Merchant, Ambassador, Historian, Author, Translator and Printer. A Monograph.* London, 1877 (reprinted in *The Library,* 2nd ser., 4 [1903], [113]–143, and also as a separate for private circulation [London, 1903].). 73

Written by a brother of William Blades for the Caxton Celebration of 1877. Follows the theory that Caxton learned printing in Cologne from Ulrich Zel (*sic*), that "it is very doubtful whether Caxton cut a single letter himself, but that, with the exception of his original fount, he imported his type from France and Holland" (p. 27, n. 1). Contains many admitted suppositions and unverified assumptions.

BLADES, WILLIAM. *The Biography and Typography of William Caxton, England's First Printer.* London, 1077. 74

This is based on and is a condensation of the same author's *Life and Typography of William Caxton* (No. 61). There was a second edition of the abridgment in 1882 (No. 92).

BLADES, WILLIAM, ed. *The Dictes and Sayings of the Philosophers. A Facsimile Reproduction of the First Book Printed in England by William Caxton, in 1477.* London, 1877. xii, facsim.   75
   A very brief introduction mentions the other two editions of the *Dictes*.
It provides the literary-historical background for the work and does not
dwell on the printing history or the printer.

BRADSHAW, HENRY. *Notice of a Fragment of the "Fifteen Oes
and Other Prayers" Printed at Westminster by W. Caxton about
1490-91. Preserved in the Library of the Baptist College, Bristol.*
London, 1877. Also in: *Collected Papers* (1889), pp. 341-349.   76
   Discusses and describes the fragment which is a cancelled copy of the
inner sheet (leaves 3, 4, 5, 6) of the first quire (sign. a) of the *Fifteen Oes
and Other Prayers*, printed by Caxton at Westminster during the years indicated. Also includes a brief discussion of printing and composing prac-
tices and methods of the incunabula period. Demonstrates that Caxton set
by formes. Calls attention to a similarly reset forme in a Wynkyn de Worde
Primer of 1494. Uses evidence from printing offsets for dating. Detailed
comments on printer's waste of Caxton, Lettou, Machlinia, Pynson, and
de Worde (*Collected Papers*, pp. 347-349).
   See also: Painter, George D. "Caxton through the Looking-Glass,"
Gutenberg Jahrbuch (No. 400), pp. 73-80.

ERNOUF, ALFRED AUGUSTE. "Causerie d'un bibliophile.
L'exposition des livres de Caxton en Angleterre." *Bulletin du
bibliophile* (1877), pp. 231-234.   77
   A brief note on the Caxton celebrations in England. Slight biographical
sketch with description of festivities.

KNIGHT, CHARLES. *William Caxton, the First English Printer: A
Biography.* London, 1877. 240 pp.   78
   See 1844 edition for details (No. 51).

MARSHALL, DAVID. *Printing. An Account of Its Invention and of
William Caxton, the First English Printer.* London and Paris,
1877.   79
   The work bears the following dedication: "To the Master, Wardens and
Assistants of the Worshipful Company of Mercers of the City of London.
This Memorial of William Caxton, one of their most illustrious liverymen,
is with their permission respectfully inscribed by their obedient servant,
the Author."
   Chapters I–IV deal with a general history of printing and the invention
of the art.
   Chapter V, "William Caxton" (pp. [55]–81), follows Blades in suppos-
ing that Caxton "acquired his knowledge of typography in Bruges and from
Colard Mansion."

POWELL, ARTHUR C. J. *A Short History of the Art of Printing in England.* London, 1877. 50 pp. (Issued as a Supplement to the Printers' Register in Commemoration of the Four Hundredth Anniversary of the Introduction of Printing into England.) 80

Chapter II: "The Introduction of Printing into England" (pp. 7–16). A well-written account which rejects the theory that the Oxford Book was the first book printed in England. Follows Blades in rejecting the proposition that Caxton learned printing in Cologne.

Chapter III: "Caxton's Contemporaries and Successors" (pp. 17–19). Follows Blades and presents no alternate theories.

PRICE, FRANCIS COMPTON, ed. *Facsimiles Illustrating the Labours of William Caxton at Westminster, and the Introduction of Printing into England. With a Memoir of Our First Printer and Bibliographical Particulars of the Illustrations.* London, 1877. 6 pp., 10 facsim. 81

Follows Blades in biographical details. Excellent facsimiles.

QUANTIN, ALBERT. *Les origines de l'imprimerie et son introduction en Angleterre d'après de récentes publications anglaises.* Paris, 1877. 70 pp. 82

Only Chapter V, "William Caxton" (pp. 53–70), deals with printing in England. Follows Blades in essentials. Makes some slight evaluation of Caxton's literary style.

SOUTHWARD, JOHN. *Four Centuries of Printing in England.* London, 1877. 83

Not examined.

SPRINGER, JOHN. *A Few Preliminary Thoughts Toward an Essay on the Life and Character of William Caxton, the First English Printer.* Iowa City, 1877. (Read before the Irving Institute of the Iowa State University, Friday Evening, February 2d, 1877.) 84

A brief attempt at an evaluation of Caxton's contribution. The author makes no reference to Blades's work, and does not seem to be familiar with any of the more recent scholarship on his subject. Believes that Caxton probably learned printing from Wynkyn de Worde and Richard Pynson; does not, however, give any evidence or reason for this supposition.

The obvious lack of true perspective and perception on the author's part is evidenced by the following statement in the opening paragraph: "He [Caxton] may be called the one great man of England – for he was the leader in the introduction into that country of the mysterious art that has raised to the commercial and brain supremacy of the globe, an island little larger than the State of Iowa; it was he who put his hand to that mysterious calling no Englishman had touched before him" (p. [3]).

ASPLAND, ALFRED, ed.   *The Golden Legend. A Reproduction from a Copy in the Manchester Free Library.* London, 1878. 44 pp. (The Holbein Society's Facsimile Reprints 13.)   85
>   Contains a brief chronology of the development of printing in the 15th century.

MADDEN, JOHN PATRICK AUGUSTE.   *Lettres d'un bibliographe,* 5e série, lettre 15: *Caxton et son apprentissage.* Paris, 1878.   86
>   Here the author denies that Caxton learned printing at Bruges.

BEEDHAM, BRAILSFORD HARRY.   *A List of Reproductions, Both Imitation and in Facsimile, of the Press of William Caxton, England's First Printer. With Some Preliminary Observations.* New York, Iowa City, 1879. xii, 24 pp.   87
>   The American edition carries a florid, moralizing "Note to the American Edition" by John Springer (see No. 84, the earlier entry under Springer). The factual content of this note is based on Blades.
>   The text of the main body of the book supplies detailed bibliographical information on Caxton reproductions extant and known at the time (1879) together with historical and technical discussions of the originals.

NOBLE, THEOPHILUS CHARLES.   *A Caxton Memorial; Extracts from the Churchwarden's Accounts of the Parish of St. Margaret, Westminster, Illustrating the Life and Times of William Caxton, the First English Printer, 1478–1492.* [London, 1880]. 32 pp. (Reprinted from *The Builder,* August 7 and 21, 1880. "For Private Circulation Only.")   88
>   Also published without author's name and with the notation about private circulation omitted.
>   Considers 1471 as the date of the introduction of printing to England. Presents a brief biographical sketch of Caxton, partially constructed on the St. Margaret parish register, which also contains entries about John Milton and Sir Walter Raleigh. Through this device the author wishes to place Caxton on the same level as these two men.

WATKINS, M. G., ed.   *A Treatyse of Fysshynge wyth an Angle, by Dame Juliana Berners: Being a Facsimile Reproduction of the First Book on the Subject of Fishing Printed in England by Wynkyn de Worde at Westminster in 1496. With an Introduction by Rev. M. G. Watkins.* London, 1880. xiv, 23 pp.   89
>   A very fine facsimile. The introduction is limited to a discussion of fishing and does not touch on the printing of this work except very cursorily.

BLADES, WILLIAM, ed.   *"The Boke of Saint Albans" by Dame Juliana Berners; Containing Treatises on Hawking, Hunting, and*

*Cote Armour. Printed at Saint Albans by the Schoolmaster-Printer
in 1486. Reproduced in Facsimile. With an Introduction by William
Blades.* London, 1881. 82 pp.   90
     Subsequent editions in 1899 and 1905.
     Introduction. Chapter I: "Authorship" (pp. [7]–15). Reviews earlier
attempts to determine the author. Finds much of the presumed evidence to
have been invented or to have been copied. Bases his views on external
as well as internal evidence.
     Chapter II: "Typography and Bibliography" (pp. [16]–23). Attempts to
identify and describe the printer and to develop his background, although
he makes no attempt to name him. Blades does not think that he was connected with either the Abbey or Caxton. List of editions of the work is on
pp. 22–23.
     Chapter III: "The Subjects Treated" (pp. [25]–28). A brief synopsis of
each of the topics treated in the book.
     Chapter IV: "Philology" (pp. [29]–32). Rather limited in scope. Deals
exclusively with orthographic peculiarities. Includes a list of particularly
striking examples.

HERRTAGE, SIDNEY J. H., ed.   *The Lyf of the Noble and Crysten
Prynce, Charles the Grete. Translated from the French by William
Caxton and Printed by Him 1485. Edited Now for the First Time,
from the Unique Copy in the British Museum.* London, 1881. xii,
268 pp. (Early English Text Society. Extra Series, Nos. 36–37.) 91
     The brief introduction (pp. v–xii) is of little value beyond establishing
the basic description of Caxton's book and providing some slight historical
background for the work. There are some negative comments on Caxton's
style in this translation.

BLADES, WILLIAM.   *The Biography and Typography of William
Caxton, England's First Printer.* 2nd ed., London, New York, 1882.
xii, 387 pp.   92
     The 1882 edition, with the exception of some slight revisions and addi-
tions, is the same as the 1877 edition. This is still the basic work on
Caxton. An extensive appendix discusses and describes each of Caxton's
publications in detail. In some respects, however, the original 2-volume
quarto edition of Blades (1861–1863) was not superseded by the later corrected condensations, as for example in the facsimiles of the assembled
alphabets of Caxton's type founts.

RICHARDSON, OCTAVIA, ed.   *The Right Plesaunt and Goodly
Historie of the Foure Sonnes of Aymon. Englisht from the French
by William Caxton, and Printed by Him About 1489.* [In two parts.]
London, 1885. (Early English Text Society. Extra Series, Nos.
44–45.)   93
     In the edition examined the introduction precedes Part II and is bound
between pp. 320 and 321 of the text. Contains brief comments on the liter-

alness of the translation (p. viii). Caxton's morphology and orthography are discussed briefly (pp. viii–xi). Description of the Caxton printing (pp. xi–xii). Glossary (pp. 593–624). "Name Index" (pp. 625–667).

FERGUSON, JOHN. "On a Copy of Albertus Magnus' *De secretis mulierum*, Printed by Machlinia." *Archaeologia: or Miscellaneous Tracts Relating to Antiquity*, 49, pt. 2 (1886), 335–343.   94
   The author sets out to prove that this particular imprint is properly attributed to Machlinia. He does this by comparing the book with other imprints from Machlinia's press.

HORSTMAN, CARL, ed.   *The Life of Saint Werburge of Chester, by Henry Bradshaw. Englisht A.D. 1513; Printed by Pynson A.D. 1521, and now Re-edited.* London, 1887. xl, 222 pp. (Early English Text Society. Original Series, No. 88.)   95
   The introduction treats the literary, historical, religious, and linguistic background of the work. No reference to the printing history other than the fact that Pynson printed it.

REED, TALBOT BAINES.   *A History of the Old English Letter Foundries, with Notes, Historical and Biographical, on the Rise and Progress of English Typography.* London, 1887.   96
   A general history of the subject, including the 15th-century beginnings of printing in England. A modern edition of this classic, revised and enlarged by A. F. Johnson, appeared in London in 1952 (No. 344).

BRADSHAW, HENRY. [A Letter to J. J. Green.] In G. W. Prothero. *A Memoir of Henry Bradshaw.* London, 1888. pp. 366–368. 97
   The letter is dated August 18, 1882. Contains an analysis of Wynkyn de Worde's type characteristics and printing habits for use in dating de Worde's books.

FURNIVALL, FREDERICK J., ed.   *The Curial Made by Maystere Alain Charretier. Translated thus in Englyssh by William Caxton, 1484. Collated with the French Original by Prof. Paul Meyer.* London, 1888. (Early English Text Society. Extra Series, No. 56.) viii, 20 pp.   98
   "Forewords" (pp. v–viii). A very slight introduction concerned briefly with literary evaluation. The text is based on the copy owned by the British Museum. The editor simply quotes Blades's second edition (No. 92) regarding *The Curial.* Supplies some marginal notes and footnotes.
   "Introduction to the *Balade*," by Prof. Paul Meyer (pp. 17–18). This is a brief note on the *balade* that is printed with Caxton's translation on p. 19.
   Glossary (p. 20).

BRADSHAW, HENRY. "Notice of a Fragment of the *Fifteen Oes and Other Prayers* Printed at Westminster by W. Caxton About 1490–91. Preserved in the Library of the Baptist College, Bristol." *Collected Papers*. Cambridge [Eng.], 1889. pp. [341]-349. Published also separately, London, 1877 (No. 76).   99

BRADSHAW, HENRY. "On the Earliest English Engravings of the Indulgence Known as the 'Image of Pity.'" *Collected Papers*. Cambridge [Eng.], 1889. pp. [84]-100. (A communication read before the Cambridge Antiquarian Society, February 25, 1867; see also No. 102).   100
    Contains a succinct account of the first four English presses, their initial letters, books, illustrations, and printers' devices. The author traces here four woodcut engravings pertaining to this indulgence and thus to the St. Gregory legend. All four were connected with Caxton's shop at Westminster. The engravings are described in great detail. The author outlines a proposal for a detailed study of woodcut engravings used in early English printing.

BRADSHAW, HENRY. "On the Engravings Fastened into the Lambeth Copy of the Salisbury Primer or *Horae* Printed by Wynkyn de Worde (about 1494)." *Collected Papers*. Cambridge [Eng.], 1889. pp. 256–257.   101
    Description of three engravings, two woodcuts and one a copper engraving, included in the work cited in the title.

BRADSHAW, HENRY. "On Two Engravings on Copper, by G. M., a Wandering Flemish Artist of the XV–XVIth Century." *Collected Papers*. Cambridge [Eng.], 1889. pp. 247–259. (Read before the Cambridge Antiquarian Society, Nov. 21, 1870.)   102
    Concerns, inter alia, some engravings fastened into the Lambeth copy of the Salisbury Primer or *Horae* printed by Wynkyn de Worde about 1494. G. M. was an engraver from Mechlin.

DUFF, EDWARD GORDON. "A New English XVth Century Printer." *The Library*, 1 (1889), 102–105.   103
    Finds the initials I H on the same page as the colophon in a copy of *Questiones Alberti de modis significandi* and in a fragment of a second 15th-century book. Hypothesizes that I H was associated with Notary, but can only speculate on the identity of the printer.

MADAN, FALCONER. "Some Curiosities of the Oxford Press." *The Library*, 1 (1889), 154–160.   104
    Only the first part, "The Expositio Hieronymi, 1468," is of primary interest here. Madan, though not flatly rejecting the generally accepted contention (see Blades and Bradshaw) that the 1468 date is an error, wishes to leave the question open on the basis of rather selective evidence.

SOMMER, OSKAR H., ed.   *"Le morte Darthur" by Syr Thomas
Malory. Faithfully Reprinted from the Original Edition (1485) of
William Caxton.* 3 vols. London, 1889–1891.   105
   Vol. I: The text.
   Vol. II: Introduction.
      1: "Sir Thomas Malory and the Various Editions of 'Le morte
Darthur'" (pp. 1–14). Caxton's 1485 printing and Wynkyn de Worde's 1498
and 1529 editions are described and discussed.
      2: "Relation of the Different Editions of 'Le morte Darthur' to Each
Other" (pp. 15–17). Concludes that de Worde's 1498 edition was printed
from Caxton's edition. Believes that de Worde's 1529 imprint is a reprint
of his own earlier one.
      3: "The Present Edition" (pp. 17–21). A fairly detailed description
and discussion of the Caxton edition and its type.
      4: "List of Errors, Omissions, and Orthographical Irregularities in
Caxton's Impression" (pp. 21–25). Lists these by page and line number.
      5: "Result of the Collation of Whittaker's Facsimiles with the Origi-
nal Pages" (pp. 26–28).
      6: "Notes on the Language of 'Le morte Darthur'" (pp. 28–42).
Fairly detailed analysis of Caxton's syntax, morphology, and orthography.
      7: "List of Various Readings Between Caxton's and Wynkyn de
Worde's Editions" (pp. 43–145). Considers the Wynkyn de Worde text of
1529 as the superior "both in exactness and correctness." Asserts that
de Worde's changes were made to modernize the text and make it more
readable. Beginning with p. 44 there is an extensive listing, book by
book, of the variants, excluding most of those that are purely orthographic.
      8: "List of Names and Places" (pp. 147–183).
      9: Glossary (pp. 185–230).
   Vol. III. "Studies on the Sources." A scholarly investigation of the
literary history and the folkloristic aspects of the Arthurian legends.

BLADES, WILLIAM.   *The Use and Development of Signatures in
Books.* Number I of his *Biographical Miscellanies.* London, 1890.
27 pp.   106
   A general, brief discussion of the use of signatures in MSS and early
printed books. Includes Caxton's use of signatures.

CULLEY, W. T. and FURNIVALL, F. J., eds.   *Caxton's "Eneydos," 1490. Englisht from the French "Liure des Eneydos," 1483.
With a Sketch of the Old French "Roman d'Énéas," by Dr. Salverda
de Grave.* London, 1890. xxxii, 214 pp. (Early English Text Society. Extra Series, No. 57.)   107
   Preface (pp. v–xix). Written by Culley. Confines itself almost exclusively to literary and linguistic problems. Comments briefly on Caxton's
style and blames the French original for much of the tautology.
   "Afterwords by F. J. Furnivall" (pp. xx–xxiii). Makes brief comments
on Caxton's style.
   "On the *Eneydes* and the *Roman d'Énéas*," by Dr. Salverda de Grave

(pp. xxiv–xxviii). Comes to the conclusion that there is no direct connection between Caxton's *Eneydos* and the *Roman d'Énéas*. This brief essay mainly compares the latter with other versions of Virgil's work.

"The Italian Prose Version of 1476" (pp. xxix–xxxii).

Index (pp. 167–187).

"Collation with Mr. Alfred H. Huth's Copy of the French Original, 1483" (pp. 188–214).

DUFF, EDWARD GORDON.   "Frederick Egmondt, an English Fifteenth Century Stationer." *The Library*, 2 (1890), 210-216.   108
Egmondt's name appears for the first time in 1493 in the colophon of the York Breviary. He was primarily an importer of books into England, having them printed in Venice – by Johannes Herzog, whose real name was Johannes Hamman – and in France. Very little biographical information on Egmondt is available. There is evidence that Egmondt also engaged in bookbinding. He seems to have been one of the prime importers of books printed at his own expense. For other information on Egmondt see Duff (No. 160), pp. 419–420.

KELLNER, LEON, ed.   *Caxton's "Blanchardyn and Eglantine,"*
c. 1489. From Lord Spencer's Unique Copy, Completed by the Original French and the Second English Version of 1595. London, 1890.
(Early English Text Society. Extra Series, No. 58.) cxxvi, 242 pp.
109
Introduction. Parts I, II, and III treat syntax and word order in Caxton's work in some detail (pp. v–cx).

Appendix. I: "Caxton as a Translator. His Style" (pp. cx–cxvi). Recognizes Caxton's abilities as a translator despite the frequency of tautological expressions, literal translations, and the like. Considers his style equal to Peacock's and thus typical of the 15th century. II: "The Manuscript and Prints of the Romance" (pp. cxvi–cxxvi).

BLADES, WILLIAM.   *The Pentateuch of Printing, with a Chapter
on Judges. With a Memoir of the Author, and List of His Works, by
Talbot B. Reed.* London, 1891. xxvi, 117 pp.   110
Intended as a popular summary of the invention and spread of printing. Of particular interest is the bibliography of Blades's works compiled by T. B. Reed.

Caxton section (pp. 32–40).

"List of Published Works by William Blades" (pp. xix–xx).

"List of Fugitive Pieces and Contributions to Periodicals" (pp. xxi–xxiv). In this list are found the following three pertinent titles, cited as they are listed by Reed and not further noted in this compilation:

1. "The First Printing Press in England." *Bookworm (Berjeau)*, Oct. 1869. "Calls attention to the technical errors and anachronisms of the pictorial representations of Caxton's first printing office."

2. "The First Printing Press at Oxford." *Antiquary*, July 1881. [With an account of the 'Exposicio' of "1468," and a list of early Oxford types.]

3. "On Caxton's 'Four Sons of Aymon.'" *Athenaeum*, April 14th, 1882.

HOLTHAUSEN, F., ed. *Infantia salvatoris.* Halle, 1891. xi,
24 pp.   111
   The primary interest of the editor is the text. Although based on Caxton's printing, the book cannot be used as a reflection of Caxton's work.
The editor notes in the introduction that he made many editorial changes in
orthography, e.g. elimination of abbreviations and normalization of spelling
generally. The foreword does not present anything of interest to the
scholar. The work is included here only because it is based on a Caxton
imprint.

RÖMSTEDT, HERMANN. *Die englische Schriftsprache bei Cax-*
ton. Göttingen, 1891. v, 54 pp. (Am 4. Juni 1880 von der philoso-
phischen Fakultät der Universität Göttingen gekrönte Preisschrift).
                                                                                      112
   An immensely detailed and thorough examination and study of Caxton's
orthography and grammatical style. Includes also comparisons and sound
analyses. Examines the various letters and sounds and their combinations
as well as the classifications of words.
   Compares, partially in tabular form, Caxton's printed version with the
same words in Chaucer, in various MSS, and in the Folio edition of Shakespeare's works. Though somewhat dated in terminology and method, the
work can still be greatly useful to the philologist and linguist.

BULLEN, GEORGE. *Sex quam elegantissimae epistolae; Printed*
by William Caxton in 1483: Reproduced in Facsimile by James
Hyatt. London, 1892.   113
   Not examined.

CLARK, J. SCOTT. *Caxton and Daniel Selections. Being Ex-*
tracts from Caxton's Prefaces, and Daniel's "Musophilus." New
York, 1892. 48 pp. (English Classic Series, No. 99.)   114
   A very brief biographical introduction (pp. 3–4) credits Mansion with
having been Caxton's instructor in the art of printing. "Extracts from Caxton's Prefaces" (pp. 5–19) are in modernized English. The volume is of
no particular significance either as a compilation or a scholarly work.

NICHOLSON, EDWARD W. B., ed. *Caxton's Advertisement. Pho-*
tolithograph of the Copy Preserved in the Bodleian Library, Oxford,
Being One of the Two Only Copies Known. London, [1892].
7 pp.   115
   The advertisement reproduced here does not bear a printer's name, date
of imprint, or place of imprint. It is, however, clearly in Caxton's type 3.
The introduction discusses the dating, language, orthography, and subject
matter of the six-line advertisement.

COLVIN, MARY NOYES, ed. *Godeffroy of Boloyne; or, The Siege*
and Conqueste of Jerusalem, by William, Archbishop of Tyre.

Translated from the French by Caxton, and Printed by Him in 1481.
London, 1893. xii, 348 pp. (Early English Text Society. Extra
Series, No. 64.) 116

Only the first section of the introduction, "Caxton's Text and Its Origi-
nal" (pp. vii–ix), is pertinent to Caxton as either printer or translator.
The editor cites Blades's 1879 edition on the description of the British
Museum copy which was used for this edition.

Because of textual peculiarities in Caxton's translation and in a French
MS edition of the 15th century (MS. 68 of the Bibliothèque Nationale),
which was formerly in the possession of Caxton's contemporary in Bruges,
Louis de Bruges, Seigneur de la Gruythuyse, the editor feels that Caxton
translated from this French copy.

"Notes" (pp. 313–316). Vocabulary (pp. 317–330). "Index of Names"
(pp. 331–341). "Index of Places" (pp. 343–348).

DUFF, EDWARD GORDON. *Early Printed Books.* London, New
York, 1893. xii, 219 pp. 117

Chapter VI: "The Low Countries" (pp. 95–112). Briefly discusses Caxton and Colard Mansion at Bruges (pp. 105–106). Refers only to historical
and biographical details. No discussion of the books printed there.

Chapter VIII: "Caxton – Wynkyn de Worde – Julian Notary" (pp. 125–146).
Considers it probable that Caxton learned printing at Cologne. Biographical data together with some description and discussion of the books.

Chapter IX: "Oxford and St. Albans" (pp. 147–159). Assumes the *Expositio* to have been printed in 1478. Follows the same pattern of discussion
as in Chapter VIII.

Chapter X: "London. John Lettou, William de Machlinia, Richard Pynson" (pp. 160–173). As in preceding chapters.

DUFF, EDWARD GORDON. "England," *Early Illustrated Books·
A History of the Declaration and Illustration of Books in the 15th
and 16th Centuries,* ed. by Alfred W. Pollard. London, 1893. Chapter XI, pp. 219–248. 118

A brief discussion of the woodcut illustrations in early English printing. Takes up the 15th century on pp. 219–229. Intended primarily for the
layman.

DUFF, EDWARD GORDON, ed. *Information for Pilgrims unto the
Holy Land. Facsimile of the Edition of W. de Worde, Westminster,
1498.* London, 1893. 119

Pages vii–xvii of Duff's introduction are devoted to historical and literary matters. Pages xvii–xx deal with background on Wynkyn de Worde and
contain a detailed description of each of three extant copies of the *Information* printed by de Worde.

PRIDEAUX, SARAH T. *An Historical Sketch of Bookbinding.*

With a Chapter on Early Stamped Bindings by E. Gordon Duff. London, 1893. 303 pp.   120
    English 15th-century bindings are discussed only briefly (pp. 14–17).

SOMMER, H. OSKAR, ed.   *The Recuyell of the Historyes of Troy,
Written in French by Raoul Lefèvre, Translated and Printed by William Caxton, (about A.D. 1474).* 2 vols. London, 1894.   121
    On title page: "The first English printed book, now faithfully reproduced with a critical introduction, index and glossary and eight pages in photographic facsimile."
    This edition contains a literal reprint of the Caxton translation. The extensive introduction deals with the literary, linguistic, and printing background of this first Caxton. The following sections are particularly pertinent:
    "William Caxton's 'The Recuyell of the Historyes of Troye,' and Colard Mansion's 'Le Recueil des Histoires de Troyes' " (pp. lxxxii–xciii).
    "Wynkyn de Worde's, Robert Copland's and the Later Editions of 'The Recuyell' " (pp. xciv–cvii).
    "The Relationship of the Various English Editions of 'The Recuyell' to one Another" (pp. cviii–cxii).
    All these sections of the introduction include fairly detailed descriptions and discussions of the particular copies involved. Though somewhat dated, the introductory material together with the reprint makes this a still valuable source book. The editor has a very low opinion of Caxton's style and use of the English language, thus reflecting the general view prevalent at the turn of the century.

MADAN, FALCONER.   *The Early Oxford Press. A Bibliography
of Printing and Publishing at Oxford, "1468"–1640.* Volume I of
Oxford Books: A Bibliography of Printed Works Relating to the University and City of Oxford or Printed or Published There. 3 vols.
Oxford, 1895–1931.   122
    "The Fifteenth Century Press" (pp. 1–4). Lists and describes the imprints of the period. Arrangement is chronological by date of imprint.
    "Appendix A, The Fifteenth Century Press" (pp. [237]–262). Includes: "The Type and Press-work" (pp. 241–244); "Watermarks" (pp. 244–245); and "Separate Books" (pp. 245–262). This appendix is supplementary to pp. 1–4 and contains extremely detailed descriptions of the imprints.
    Although the author is inclined to accept the "1468" date of imprint as an error, he does not consider the arguments against this date as completely conclusive and still prefers to leave the date of the first Oxford Book as at least slightly doubtful.
    The book is an essential and important source for information on the title subject.

ALLNUTT, W. H.   "English Provincial Presses, 1478–1556."
Bibliographica. Papers on Books, Their History and Art, 2, Part 1
(1896), 23–46.   123

I: "Oxford, '1468' to 1486." Assumes "1468" date to be an error and considers Caxton to have been the first printer in England. Lists Oxford imprints chronologically during the period stated.

II: "St. Albans, 1480-1486." Raises the possibility that the Schoolmaster Printer learned his art at Caxton's office due to the close similarity of the St. Albans type with Caxton's type 2*. Lists known issues of the press.

The foregoing are the only 15th-century presses discussed.

DUFF, EDWARD GORDON. *Early English Printing. A Series of Facsimiles of All the Types Used in England during the XVth Century, with Some of Those Used in the Printing of English Books Abroad.* London, 1896. viii, 40 pp.   124

Whole-page facsimiles of every 15th-century English type. The reproductions are as near full size as possible. The plates are described separately, followed by a "Table of English Type" arranged by press or printer with dates given. The following are represented: (1) William Caxton; (2) Wynkyn de Worde; (3) Julian Notary; (4) Lettou and Machlinia; (5) printer of Caoursin' *Siege of Rhodes*; (6) Richard Pynson; (7) the Oxford Press; (8) St. Albans Press; (9) foreign printers.

DZIATSKO, KARL. "Warum Caxton Buchdrucker wurde." *Beiträge zur Kenntnis des Schrift-, Buch- und Bibliothekswesens*, 3 (1896), 8-23. (Sammlung bibliothekswissenschaftlicher Arbeiten, 10.)   125

Not examined.

POLLARD, ALFRED W. *Facsimiles from Early Printed Books in the British Museum. Selected Pages from Representative Specimens of the Early Printed Books of Germany, Italy, France, Holland, and England, Exhibited in the King's Library.* London, 1897.   126

Thirty-two plates, including facsimiles of Caxton, Wynkyn de Worde, Pynson, the Printer of St. Albans, and the Oxford Press. Also contains descriptions of the plates. Primarily of value to the student of typography.

STRACHEY, SIR EDWARD, ed. *Le morte Darthur. Sir Thomas Malory's Book of King Arthur and His Noble Knights of the Round Table: The Text of Caxton.* London, New York, 1897.   127

"William Caxton" (pp. xxviii-xxx) of the introduction. This is a brief biographical sketch following Blades.

"The Text and Its Several Editions" (pp. xxxi-xxxvii). A brief comparison of the various editions. Gives only the most cursory background.

PLOMER, HENRY R. "New Documents on English Printers and Booksellers of the Sixteenth Century." *The Bibliographical Society. Transactions*, 4 (London, 1898 [for 1896-98]), 154-183.   128

Although dealing exclusively with the 16th century, this article is nevertheless included because of the several printers whose lives and work started in the preceding century. The article includes the Star Chamber proceedings for the reign of Henry VIII that involved Pynson (pp. 154–155 and 165–166).

[AMES, JOSEPH]. *An Index to Dibdin's Edition of the "Typographical Antiquities" First Compiled by Joseph Ames. With Some References to the Intermediate Edition by William Herbert.* London, 1899.   129
Issued separately in this reprint.

BLADES, WILLIAM, ed. *"The Boke of Saint Albans" by Dame Juliana Berners; Containing Treatises on Hawking, Hunting, and Cote Armour. Printed at Saint Albans by the Schoolmaster-Printer in 1486. Reproduced in Facsimile.* London, 1899.   130
For details see entry under first edition (No. 90).

BUTLER, PIERCE. *Legenda Aurea– Légende Doré– Golden Legend. A Study of Caxton's "Golden Legend" with Special Reference to Its Relations to the Earlier English Prose Translations.* Baltimore, 1899. vi, 154 pp. (The Johns Hopkins University, Dissertation.)   131
Primarily a detailed textual criticism involving the evolution of the legend in its various forms up to the time of Caxton. The work is of primary interest to the literary scholar dealing with comparative problems. The different manuscript sources are closely analyzed and compared, both linguistically and literarily.

DUFF, EDWARD GORDON. *The Printers, Stationers, and Bookbinders of London and Westminster in the Fifteenth Century.* Aberdeen [Scot.], 1899. 105 pp. (The Sandars Lectures for 1899.)   132
These lectures were later combined with the Sandars Lectures for 1904 by the same author and published under the title *The Printers, Stationers and Bookbinders of Westminster and London from 1476 to 1535* (No. 157).
Lecture I, "The Printers at Westminster," covers Caxton, de Worde, and Notary.
Lecture II, "The Printers at London," discusses Lettou, Machlinia, and Pynson.
Lecture III, "The Stationers," discusses books printed abroad for the English market and the stationers who sold them.
Lecture IV, "The Bookbinders."

BRADLEY, HENRY, ed. *Dialogues in French and English. Edited from Caxton's Printed Text (about 1483), with an Introduction,*

Notes and Word List. London, 1900. xii, 78 pp. (Early English
Text Society. Extra Series, No. 79.) 133
The work is also known under the following titles: *A Book for
Travellers* and *A Vocabulary in French and English.* It was
adapted from *Le livre des mestiers: Dialogues français-flamands
composées au XIV siècle par un maitre d'école de la ville de
Bruges.*
The text for the EETS edition is based on the copy in the library of
Ripon Cathedral. The work itself is largely a collection of colloquial
phrases and dialogues. The date of its printing is inferred by Blades on
the basis of the type used.
The introduction (pp. v–x) has the oft-repeated shortsighted commentary
on Caxton's "servile translations." Makes some textual comparisons with
the French edition.
Notes (pp. xi–xii).
"List of English Words" (pp. 53–60).
"Names of People, Places, etc." (pp. 61–63).
"List of French Words" (pp. 64–78).

JENKINS, R. "Early Attempts at Paper-making in England, 1495–
1586." *Library Association Record,* 2 (1900), 479–488. 134
A brief biographical outline of the papermakers during the period indicated in the title. Of these only John Tate is pertinent to this listing.
The author says Wynkyn de Worde printed on Tate's paper.

PLOMER, HENRY R. *A Short History of English Printing, 1476–
1900.* London, 1900. xv, 330 pp. 135
Chapter I: "Caxton and His Contemporaries" (pp. 1–26). Author follows Duff's theory that Caxton printed a Bartholomaeus Anglicus in Cologne. Bases this in part on de Worde's oft-cited colophon to his edition
of Bartholomaeus. The chapter gives a brief, concise account of 15th-cen-
tury printing.
Chapter II: "From 1501 to the Death of Wynkyn de Worde" (pp. 27–49).
This chapter is cited here largely for the sake of continuity since de Worde
and other printers of incunabula extended their activity beyond the turn of
the century.

DUFF, EDWARD GORDON, ed. *Commemoracio lamentacionis siue
compassionis Beate Marie. Reproduced in Facsimile from the
Unique Copy Printed at Westminster by William Caxton.* Oxford,
1901. x, 63 pp. 136
The introduction very briefly discusses the typographical and historical
background of this work.

POLLARD, ALFRED W. *English Literature. William Caxton.*
Philadelphia, 1901. 15 pp. (Reprinted from *Chambers's Cyclopae-
dia of English Literature.* New edition [1901]–1902.) 137

In this brief essay Pollard evaluates Caxton's contribution to literature. He thinks Caxton was a man of literary tastes and skill as well as a highly competent businessman.

REAUL, PAUL DE. *The Language of Caxton's "Reynard the Fox."* A Study in Historical English Syntax. Ghent, London, 1901. xvii, 233 pp. (Université de Gand. Recueil de Travaux publié par la Faculté de Philosophie et Lettres. 26e fascicule.)   138
A detailed study of grammatical syntax in Caxton, examining one by one the various parts of speech, tenses, cases, and the like. Only peripheral reference to Caxton's style, and then only in the context of grammatical syntax. A precise, scholarly, but somewhat narrow study.

SHAW, A. E. "The Earliest Latin Grammars in English." *The Bibliographical Society.* Transactions, 5 (London, 1901 [for 1898–1900]), 39–65.   139
Contains some brief references to books printed by Wynkyn de Worde, Pynson, and Rood. The main emphasis of the article is on the contents rather than on printing.

KENNARD, JOSEPH S. *Some Early Printers and Their Colophons.* Philadelphia, 1902.   140
A brief, sentimentalized discussion. Caxton (pp. 103–118); Wynkyn de Worde (p. 119).

BLADES, ROWLAND HILL. "Who Was Caxton?" *The Library*, 2nd ser., 4 (1903), [113]–143.   141
Originally issued in 1877 as a monograph (see No. 73).

GIBSON, STRICKLAND. *Early Oxford Bindings.* Oxford, 1903. 69 pp., 40 plates. (Bibliographical Society. Illustrated Monographs, 10.)   142
Treats only decorated bindings.
Introduction (pp. 1–13). A brief general history from the middle of the 12th to the 17th century.
"I: List of Bindings. Stamped Bindings, Grouped Chronologically" (pp. 15–25). Lists 32 bindings, described in detail, which were bound prior to 1500.
"II: Chronological List of Oxford Binders, c. 1180–1640." Binders active in the 15th century are listed on pp. 45–46.

PLOMER, HENRY R. *Abstracts from the Wills of English Printers and Stationers, from 1492–1630.* London, 1903. v, 67 pp.   143
Only the wills of Pynson and Wynkyn de Worde are of specific pertinence to this listing (see pp. 3–4).

PLOMER, HENRY R. "Richard Pynson v. Henry Squyr." *The*

Bibliographical Society. Transactions, 6 (London, 1903 [for 1900–1902]), 137–141.   144
   Other documentation of this lawsuit was discussed earlier by Plomer (see No. 128).

POLLARD, ALFRED W.   "Some Notes on English Illustrated Books." *The Bibliographical Society. Transactions*, 6 (London, 1903 [for 1900–1902]), 29–[61].   145
   Includes some data and illustrations relative to Caxton, Wynkyn de Worde, and Pynson.

STEELE, ROBERT.   *The Earliest English Music Printing. A Description and Bibliography of English Printed Music to the Close of the Sixteenth Century.* London, 1903. xi, 102 pp. (The Bibliographical Society. Illustrated Monographs, 11.)   146
   The bibliography (pp. 33ff.) lists three works printed prior to 1500; also several by Pynson and Wynkyn de Worde in the first part of the 16th century. Figs. 1–6 illustrate the work of Pynson and de Worde.

GASQUET, F. A.   "The Bibliography of Some Devotional Books Printed by the Earliest English Printers." *The Bibliographical Society. Transactions*, 7 (London, 1904 [for 1902–1904]), 163–189.   147
   Covers the period up to 1510. Primarily a listing of books dealing with religion and religious subjects. Divided by categories. Gives date of imprint and printer when known. Includes the printers of incunabula, much of whose production had a religious orientation.

GRAY, GEORGE J.   *The Earlier Cambridge Stationers and Bookbinders and the First Cambridge Printer.* Oxford, 1904. 81 pp. (The Bibliographical Society. Illustrated Monographs, 13.)   148
   Part I: "To the End of the Fifteenth Century" (pp. 1–17). This section is of necessity very brief and speculative since no example of the work of these men exists. The main part of the book deals with the 16th-century printers.

MADAN, FALCONER.   *A Chart of Oxford Printing, "1468"–1900. With Notes and Illustrations.* Oxford, 1904. 50 pp. (The Bibliographical Society. Illustrated Monographs, 12.)   149
   Stillwell cites a first issue of this work in 100 copies, published in 1903. The second issue, of 1904, had a printing of 425 copies, slightly altered and corrected.
   The work is based on a paper read before the Oxford Architectural and Historical Society, Feb. 1888 (printed in *The Library* for 1889) and on a lecture before the Bibliographical Society, Oct. 20, 1902 (printed in the *Periodical*, Dec. 1902).
   "The First Press" (pp. 13–14). List of the then known issues. The

work's pertinence to 15th-century printing is limited because of the small number of known issues and the brief period of printing in this century. Madan tentatively accepts the first Oxford Book as having been printed in 1478.

SAYLE, CHARLES.   "Initial Letters in Early English Printed Books." *The Bibliographical Society. Transactions*, 7 (London, 1904 [for 1902–1904]), 15–47.   150
  Deals primarily with the 16th century, though the discussion begins with 15th-century printers. Establishes that initial letters appeared in 1480, four years earlier than the date given by Blades in his work on Caxton. Caxton, Wynkyn de Worde, Notary, and Pynson are discussed (pp. 21–25). Well illustrated.

BLADES, WILLIAM, ed.   *"The Boke of Saint Albans" by Dame Juliana Berners* ... London, 1905. 32 pp., facsim. 175 pp.   151
  See No. 90 for description.

CRÜWELL, G. A.   "William Caxton's vroegste drukkers-werkzaam-heit." *Tijdschrift voor boek- en bibliotheekwezen*, 3 (1905), 223–236, 300–315.   152
  A fairly detailed, thorough two-part study including typography, biography, and historical and economic background.

DUFF, EDWARD GORDON.   *A Century of the English Book Trade. Short Notices of All Printers, Stationers, Book-Binders and Others Connected with It from the Issue of the First Dated Book in 1457 to the Incorporation of the Company of Stationers in 1557.* London, 1905. xxxv, 200 pp. (The Bibliographical Society. Publications, Ser. 1, No. 9.)   153
  The introduction (pp. i–xxx) presents a brief history of the English book trade as distinct from the art of printing.
  The body of the work is an alphabetical listing of printers, stationers, and binders, with brief biographical notes. It also establishes their specific connection with the English book trade. Lists foreign residents who had contact with the English book and printing market as well as English citizens and foreigners resident in England.
  Appendix I: "Index of Christian Names" (pp. 180–184).
  Appendix II: "Index of London Signs" (pp. 187–194).
  Appendix III: "Chronological Index of Foreign Places, Printers and Stationers" (pp. 197–200).

DUFF, EDWARD GORDON.   *William Caxton.* Chicago, 1905. 118 pp.   154
  Disagrees with Blades; believes that Caxton learned at least the rudiments of printing at Cologne. Assumes that Caxton first established a press in 1474 with Colard Mansion as partner and assistant. Although this

biography is, to a large part, based on Blades's work, Duff departs from the older work on the basis of subsequent research.

"List of Caxton's Books with Collation" (pp. 91–98).

POLLARD, ALFRED W. "Recent Caxtoniana." *The Library*, 2nd ser., 6 (1905), 337–353. 155

The first item discussed is an article by S. M. Peartree (No. 156) describing a possibly authentic portrait of Caxton. In this context Pollard raises the possibility that Caxton taught printing to Mansion.

The other item of Caxtoniana is Duff's *William Caxton* (No. 154), which is reviewed here.

PEARTREE, S. MONTAGUE. "A Portrait of William Caxton."
The Burlington Magazine for Connoisseurs, 7 (1905), 383–387. 156

The "portrait" in question is an engraving bound in a copy of Caxton's *Recuyell*. It shows a kneeling man presenting two books to a lady. On the basis of the author's admittedly highly speculative suppositions, it seems questionable that one can say with assurance that the engraving does indeed show Caxton. (See also Pollard, "Recent Caxtoniana," *The Library* (No. 155).

DUFF, EDWARD GORDON. *The Printers, Stationers, and Bookbinders of Westminster and London from 1476 to 1535.* Cambridge [Eng.], 1906. 256 pp. 157

This volume combines the Sandars Lectures for 1899 and 1904. For first publication of the 1899 lectures see No. 132.

SCHMERSAHL, E. "Caxton Drucke." *Börsenblatt für den deutschen Buchhandel* (1906). 158

Not examined.

VARNHAGEN, HERMANN. *Commentatio de duobus foliis libri cuiusdam anglici adhuc ignoti exeunte saeculo quinto decimo typis excusi, quae in Museo Britannico asservantur.* Erlangen, 1906. (Rektoratsprogramm von Erlangen, 1906). 159

Not examined.

DUFF, EDWARD GORDON. "Early Chancery Proceedings Concerning Members of the Book Trade." *The Library*, 2nd ser., 8 (1907), 408–420. 160

Reprints six documents pertaining to the early English book trade.

No. 1 (p. 412) pertains to a debt owed by Caxton.

No. 2 (pp. 413–414) involves Machlinia's *Nova Statuta* and helps confirm the imprint date of the book.

No. 3 (pp. 414–415) involves Caxton's son-in-law and gives the name of Caxton's executor, Richard Wade.

No. 4 (pp. 416–417) presents an action against William Wilcock, who commissioned the two books printed by Lettou between 1480 and 1481.

No. 5 (pp. 417–419) involves Joyce Pelgrim, a London bookseller.

No. 6 (pp. 419–420) brings together Ravynell, Joyce, and Egmont (*sic*), all three early stationers.

DUFF, EDWARD GORDON. "Richard Pynson and Thomas Bercula." *The Library*, 2nd ser., 8 (1907), 298–303.   161

Seeks to establish a connection between Pynson and Thomas Bercula. The sudden and drastic improvements in the appearance and character of Pynson's imprints in 1518, Duff surmises, must have been due to heavy financial support. He assumes that this came from Bercula. He also makes quite a good case for the theory that the draper Bartellet, the printer Barthelet, and Bercula were the same person.

GIBSON, STRICKLAND. *Abstracts from the Wills and Testamentary Documents of Binders, Printers, and Stationers of Oxford, from 1493 to 1638.* London, 1907. xxiii, 61 pp. (The Bibliographical Society. Publications, Ser. 1, No. 10.)   162

The introduction (pp. xv–xxiii) is a brief historical statement. Only one 15th-century will is listed, that of John Bray, bookbinder (p. 1).

Appendix B: "Alphabetical List of Binders, Printers and Stationers of Oxford, 1457–1640" (pp. 40–54).

DUFF, EDWARD GORDON. "English Fifteenth Century Broadsides." *The Bibliographical Society. Transactions*, 9 (London, 1908 [for 1906–1908]), 211–227.   163

Describes and discusses indulgences printed by Caxton, Lettou, and Pynson in the years 1480, 1481, 1489, 1498, and 1499.

DUFF, EDWARD GORDON. *Horae Beate Virginis Marie secundum Sarum. The Unique Copy Printed at Westminster by William Caxton, circa 1477. A Monograph.* London, [1908]. 47 pp.   164

Pages 3–19 give a brief biography of Caxton. The remainder of the little volume is devoted to a description of the *Horae* and also to a discussion of the liturgical literature of the period.

DUFF, EDWARD GORDON. "The Introduction of Printing into England and the Early Work of the Press." *The Cambridge History of English Literature*, ed. by Sir A. W. Ward and A. R. Waller. Cambridge, 1908. Vol. II, 310–331.   165

Duff states that Caxton's first contact with printing was at Cologne in 1471 when he assisted in printing an edition of Bartholomaeus Anglicus' *De proprietatibus rerum*, that two years later he took Mansion as associate, and that it was the latter who obtained the type – probably from John Veldener of Louvain – with which Caxton began his own printing office. There follows a brief professional and personal biography of Caxton together with brief discussions of the other 15th-century printers.

By and large Duff seems not to appreciate fully Caxton's considerable contribution to English literary taste.

For a literary evaluation see, in this same volume (pp. 332–340), "English Prose in the Fifteenth Century," by Alice Greenwood.

GREENWOOD, ALICE D.   "English Prose in the Fifteenth Century; II: Caxton. Malory. Berners." *The Cambridge History of English Literature*, ed. by Sir A. W. Ward and A. R. Waller. Cambridge, 1908.   Vol. II, 332–340.   166
Does not fully appreciate Caxton's literary and linguistic contributions. Judgments and evaluations are made in the light of present-day literary values and sensitivities rather than on the basis of Caxton's impact on English literary history during and after his lifetime.

JENNINGS, OSCAR.   *Early Woodcut Initials. Containing over Thirteen Hundred Reproductions of Ornamental Letters of the Fifteenth and Sixteenth Centuries.* London, 1908.   167
Chapter XVI: "English Initials" (pp. 108a–108d). This aspect of printing was still rather undeveloped in England during the 15th century, and the subject is thus of slight importance for this period. Pertinent illustrations are found on pp. 277–280.

MADAN, FALCONER.   *A Brief Account of the University Press at Oxford; with Illustrations Together with a Chart of Oxford Printing.* Oxford, 1908.   40 pp.   168
A short treatment of the subject adding nothing not found in the author's earlier works.

BLEI, FRANZ.   "Von frühen Druckwerken und über Caxton." *Der Zwiebelfisch*, 1. Jahrg., Heft 3 (1909), 3–7.   169
A very brief and sketchy account of early printing. Follows the theory that Caxton learned printing at Cologne. The work has only slight interest.

DE RICCI, SEYMOUR.   *A Census of Caxtons.* Oxford, 1909. 196 pp. (The Bibliographical Society. Illustrated Monographs, 15.)   170
Classifies works from Caxton's press in the same order as does Duff (in *William Caxton*, No. 154). Includes some early imprints of Wynkyn de Worde, printed immediately after Caxton's death.

Provides the following information for each entry: 1, exact title; 2, collation (based on Duff); 3, references to Blades, Hain and Copinger, and Ames (all three editions); 4, list of copies when present owner is known (also past owners); 5, imperfections in copies; 6, the binding; 7, size of copy in mm.; 8, list of untraced copies; 9, list of fragments and single leaves.

"Facsimiles" following p. xv illustrate the Caxton types.

"Books Printed at Bruges" (pp. 1–8).
"Books Printed at Westminster" (pp. 9–107).
"Books Printed at Paris for Caxton" (pp. 108–109).
"Books Printed by Wynkyn de Worde after Caxton's Death but with Caxton's Types" (pp. 110–117).
"Unknown Printers" (p. 117).
"Summary Showing the Number of Copies Existing, Untraced, or Fragmentary" (pp. 119–122).
"A List of Caxton's Books Classified by Types in the Chronological Order for Each Type" (pp. 123–126).
"A List of Caxton's Books in Chronological Order Showing the Types Used in Each Year" (pp. 127–129).
"Index to Libraries Which Contain or Have Contained Caxtons" (pp. 133–196).

GUPPY, HENRY, ed. *"Propositio Johannis Russell" Printed by William Caxton circa A.D. 1476. Reproduced in Facsimile from the Copy Preserved in the John Rylands Library, Manchester.* Manchester, London, 1909. 35 pp. (The John Rylands Facsimiles, No. 1.)   171
     The brief introduction presents a history of the copy, a typographical description, and biographical data on author and printer.

PLOMER, HENRY R. "The Lawsuits of Richard Pynson." *The Library*, 2nd ser., 10 (1909), 115–133.   172
     The most interesting of these suits deals with an action brought by Pynson for recovery of money owed him for certain books. In one bill of complaint Pynson is referred to as a "bookbinder," in another as one who practices "the craft of prynting of bokys to the eruditiõn of many well disposed clerkys and lerned men."
     The suits involve *Dives and Paupers* (1493) and other books. The article is of special interest because the documents which are appended provide information on book prices and sizes of editions.

WINSHIP, GEORGE PARKER. *William Caxton. A Paper Read at a Meeting of the Club of Odd Volumes in Boston, Massachusetts, U.S.A.* [n.p.], 1909. 25 pp.   173
     A general, popularized brief biography.

MOORE, SAMUEL. "Caxton Reproductions: A Bibliography." *Modern Language Notes*, 25 (1910), 165–167.   174
     A listing of reproductions. Does not provide entries for multiple editions. Rather dated and of limited value.

VINE, GUTHRIE, ed. *A litil boke the whiche traytied and reherced many gode thinges necessaries for the Pestilence. Made by the Bisshop of Arnsiens . . . (London), (1485?). Reproduced in Facsim-*

ile from the Copy in the John Rylands Library. Manchester, London, 1910. (The John Rylands Facsimiles, No. 3.) xxxvi, facsim. 18 pp.   175

The introduction (iv–xxxvi) discusses the spread, incidence, and virulence of the plague. This is followed by a detailed study of the relationship of Lettou and Machlinia, the latter having printed the work originally.

DUFF, EDWARD GORDON. *The English Provincial Printers, Stationers and Bookbinders to 1557.* Cambridge [Eng.], 1912. ix, 153 pp. (The Sandars Lectures of 1911.)   176

A detailed study of the subject indicated in the title.

Appendix I: "List of Books Printed by Provincial Printers or for Provincial Stationers" (pp. 129–139). This listing includes a notation of the libraries at which the books were then preserved.

POLLARD, ALFRED W. "Printing in England (1476–1580)." *Fine Books.* London, 1912. pp. 204–223.   177

Follows theory that Caxton learned printing at Cologne and that he printed the *De proprietatibus rerum* in that city.

POLLARD, ALFRED W. "English Woodcut Illustrations." *Fine Books.* London, 1912. pp. 250–266.   178

General historical comments and illustrations.

POLLARD, ALFRED W. "Engraved Illustrations." *Fine Books.* London, 1912. pp. 267–296.   179

Page 272 presents an engraving, possibly used by Caxton for the *Recuyell.* The engraving may show Caxton.

MAGNIEN, C. "Une page d'histoire anglo-belge, 1441–1472? Caxton à la cour de Charles-le-Téméraire, à Bruges; introduction de l'imprimerie en Angleterre, 1472–1474." *Annuaire de la Société d'Archeologie de Bruxelles*, 23 (1912), 49–55.   180

Not examined.

WERTHER, HANS. "William Caxton, der erste englische Buchdrucker." *Allgemeine Buchhändlerzeitung*, 19 (1912), 209.   181

Not examined.

DUFF, EDWARD GORDON, *et al. Hand-List of Books Printed by London Printers, 1501–1556.* London, 1913.   182

Although beginning with the year 1501, this title needs to be included because of the printers of incunabula who continued printing in the 16th century. The 15th-century imprints of these printers are listed chronologically, as are those of the 16th century. Illustrations of printers' devices follow each printer.

Part I, by E. G. Duff, treats Wynkyn de Worde: 1493–1500 (pp. 1–5); 1501–1535 (pp. 5–26); and Julian Notary: 1496–1500 (p. 1); 1500–1520 (pp. 2–4).

Part II, by H. R. Plomer, from the notes of E. Gordon Duff, treats Richard Pynson: 1493–1500 (pp. 3–6); 1501–1530 (pp. 6–16).

As far as printers' devices are concerned, this work is superseded by the next entry, R. B. McKerrow's *Printers' and Publishers' Devices in England and Scotland.*

McKERROW, RONALD B. *Printers' and Publishers' Devices in England and Scotland, 1485–1640.* London, 1913. liv, 216 pp. (The Bibliographical Society. Illustrated Monographs, 16.)   183

Contains an account of marks and devices used by printers and publishers resident in England and Scotland within the years specified; also of woodcut borders and ornaments with owner's device or initials.

"Printers' Devices" (p. 1ff): A chronological list with detailed descriptions, measurements, and location.

The numbers provided here after each printer's name refer to the entry number in "Printers' Devices." The facsimiles bear the same number as the descriptive entries.

Caxton: 1.

Pynson: 3, 6, 9, 32, 35, 41, 44, 53.

Wynkyn de Worde: 1, 2, 10, 11, 12, 19, 20, 21, 23, 24, 25, 27, 30, 42, 46, 49, 50.

Notary: 8, 13, 26, 28.

St. Albans: 4.

MUNRO, JOHN JAMES, ed. *The History of Jason. Translated from the French of Raoul Le Fevre by William Caxton, c. 1477.* London, 1913. (Early English Text Society. Extra Series, No. 140.)   184

A brief prefatory note of no value. A promised second volume with introduction, collation, notes, and glossary has not yet appeared.

PRIOR, OLIVER H., ed. *Caxton's Mirrour of the World.* London, New York, 1913 [for 1912]. xxv, 192 pp. (Early English Text Society. Extra Series, No. 110.)   185

The copy used for the text reproduced here is in the British Museum, No. IB 55041–c. 10.6.5. The editor believes that the French MS from which Caxton worked was the British Museum MS Roy. 19A IX. The editor follows the facts and information provided by Blades and de Ricci regarding the history of Caxton's translation and printing.

Mirrour of the World was the first work printed in England to contain illustrations. It was translated in 1480 and probably printed in 1481.

"Index of Proper Names and of Subjects Dealt with in the *Mirrour*" (pp. 187–192).

CROUS, ERNST. "The Inventory of Incunabula in Great Britain and Ireland." *Bibliographical Society. Transactions*, 12 (London, 1914 [for 1911-1913]), 177-209. 186

A list of collections arranged alphabetically by location. Does not show individual incunabula nor does the compiler indicate country or place of imprint. Shows only total number held in each collection. Of limited usefulness and also quite dated.

PLOMER, HENRY R. *A Short History of English Printing, 1476-1900.* 2nd ed., London, 1915. 187

See Plomer (No. 135) for complete entry.

ALDIS, HARRY G. *The Printed Book.* Cambridge [Eng.], 1916. 188

A brief general history up to the present. English printing of the 15th century, pp. 11-20; Caxton, pp. 11-13.

Later editions in 1941 and 1951.

BOSANQUET, EUSTACE F. *English Printed Almanacks and Prognostications. A Bibliographical History to the Year 1600.* London, 1917. xi, 204 pp. (The Bibliographical Society. Illustrated Monograph, 17.) 189

Lists an almanack of 1498(?) printed by Wynkyn de Worde (item V, p. 79) and one printed by Richard Pynson (item IV, p. 79). These are the only two extant prior to 1500 except one not printed with movable type c. 1500(?) (p. 77). The following were printed by Pynson in the 16th century in the years indicated: items VI (1500), VII (1502), X_A (1520), X_B (1520). Item XII (1523) was printed by de Worde.

The author later published a series of corrections and additions, but none are pertinent to the years before 1501 (see No. 219).

CUNNINGTON, SUSAN. *The Story of William Caxton.* London, 1917. 190 pp. 190

A popularized biography giving the historical, social, and cultural background of the period. Relies mainly on Blades for biographical data.

DUFF, EDWARD GORDON. "England." *Early Illustrated Books: A History of the Declaration and Illustration of Books in the 15th and 16th Centuries,* ed. by Alfred W. Pollard. 2nd ed., rev. and corr., London, 1917. 191

See main entry No. 118.

KRUITWAGEN, P. BONAVENTURA. "Spaansche-Portugeesche en Engelsche incunabelen." *Het Boek*, 8 (1919), 97-107, 305-314, 345-356. 192

A three-part connected study of Spanish-Portuguese influence in English incunabula. Deals primarily with type design, analysis, and comparison, as well as statistical comparisons. Traces the travels of the various printers till, ultimately, they or their designs influenced English printing.

DEANSELY, MARGARET. "Vernacular Books in England in the Fourteenth and Fifteenth Centuries." *Modern Language Review,* 15 (1920), 349-358.   193

An article of fairly general scope dealing with book ownership during the 14th and 15th centuries. The information presented was obtained largely from wills and other official documents. It is primarily of cultural and social interest.

DE RICCI, SEYMOUR. "Colard Mansion." *The Library,* 4th ser., 1 (1921), 94-95.   194

Abstract of paper read before the Bibliographical Society [London] on March 22, 1920. Raises the questions posed for scholars by Mansion and his work. Does not attempt to answer them in this very brief abstract.

LATHROP, HENRY B. "The First English Printers and Their Patrons." *The Library*, 4th ser., 3 (1923), 69-96.   195

Disagrees with Duff and Blades that Caxton's books did not represent popular demands. Points out that Caxton enjoyed a high degree of patronage and also that he followed rather than initiated popular tastes by publishing editions of older works that had shown their popularity. With Wynkyn de Worde, the author contends, began a gradual shift in the printer's art to a more impersonal view, and the number of reprints increased as patronage decreased. The author believes that only the Printer of St. Albans produced largely what he liked rather than what was desired by a noble patron.

The article is a thorough, well-documented work, although it does limit Caxton's contribution somewhat.

PLOMER, HENRY R. "Richard Pynson, Glover and Printer." *The Library*, 4th ser., 3 (1923), 49-51.   196

The author discovered a "Ric[ardu]s Pynson...Glover" listed in the Public Record Office for 1482 and establishes the strong possibility that he was identical with the printer. This surmise is based largely on negative evidence, however, and cannot be considered as conclusive.

[BIRCH, J. G.]. "William Caxton's Stay at Cologne." *The Library*, 4th ser., 4 (1924), 50-52.   197

The first publication of Birch's discovery of four entries of permission for temporary residence in Cologne issued to William Caxton. These were found in the Alien Register of Cologne and are dated July 17, 1471, Aug. 9, 1471, Dec. 11, 1471, and July 19, 1472. Duff, in "Caxton on the Continent," *The Library*, 4th ser., 7 (1927), 398, points out that Birch's "information was published in an obscure footnote by Walther Stein in 1907." (Ed. note: This reference could not be found.)

GREG, WALTER W. "The Early Printed Editions of the *Canterbury Tales*." *Publications of the Modern Language Association*, 34 (1924), 737–761. 198

A detailed textual examination of the six earliest printed versions of the *Canterbury Tales*: (1) Caxton, the 1478 and 1484 imprints; (2) Pynson, the 1490 and 1526 imprints; (3) Wynkyn de Worde, the 1498 printing; and (4) Godfray, the 1532 printing.

The author takes the first 116 lines of the "Knight's Tale" and subjects them to a close comparative examination. He also uses the readings of two MS copies, one at Trinity College, Cambridge, and the other at Corpus Christi College, Oxford.

A table listing major variants, line by line, is included (pp. 744–749).

The conclusion reached here is that only Caxton's first edition was set completely from MS copy but that the five other editions also used MSS to varying degrees. "Caxton's first edition alone ranks with the manuscripts as a textual authority."

HAEBLER, KONRAD. "England, 1476–1500." *Die deutschen Buchdrucker des XV. Jahrhunderts im Auslande*. Munich, 1924, pp. 273–280. 199

Establishes a connection between Mansion and Caxton at Bruges. Holds that Caxton made use of the printing shop owned by Mansion. Contends that Wynkyn de Worde obtained his type from Dutch or French sources. Rejects Duff's idea (*q.v. Early English Printing*, 1896, p. 12) that John Lettou was identical with Johannes Bulle of Bremen.

Haebler states that the oldest Oxford imprints, those of 1478 and 1479, are printed with pronouncedly Cologne type. He thus assumes a German printer even prior to Theodoricus Rood, who favored Dutch type designs.

PLOMER, HENRY R. *English Printers' Ornaments*. London, 1924. xii, 291 pp. 200

A general work dealing with ornamentation. Points out that ornaments were unimportant to 15th-century printers. Caxton felt that the literature itself was more significant than decoration and thus paid little attention to the latter. In this he was followed by other printers of the century, none of whom had had training in art. Items 1–9 are illustrations of borders belonging to 15th-century printers.

PLOMER, HENRY R. "The Importation of Books into England in the Fifteenth and Sixteenth Centuries." *The Library*, 4th ser., 4 (1924), 146–150. 201

Provides important information on the book trade of the period. Plomer derived his information from an examination of the Customs Rolls at the Public Record Office.

PLOMER, HENRY R. *William Caxton (1424–1491)*. London, Boston, 1925. 195 pp. (The Roadmaker Series.) 202

A good general biography including descriptions of Caxton's typography.

PLOMER, HENRY R. *Wynkyn de Worde and His Contemporaries from the Death of Caxton to 1535. A Chapter in English Printing.* London, 1925. 263 pp.   203
    A detailed work including general historical information particularly pertinent to the book trade of the period.
    Includes Pynson, Lettou, Machlinia, and Notary as well as printers who did not become active until the 16th century. Contains descriptions and illustrations of type faces and of the books printed.

POLLARD, ALFRED W. "William Blades and Caxton's Work at Cologne." *Gutenberg Festschrift* (1925), pp. 237-240.   204
    On the basis of recent evidence Pollard contradicts Blades's assertion that Caxton could not have printed the *Bartholomaeus* in Cologne. Pollard thus considers Wynkyn de Worde's introduction to his own edition of the work as accurate.

AURNER, NELLIE SLAYTON. *Caxton. Mirrour of Fifteenth Century Letters. A Study of the Literature of the First English Press.* London, 1926. Boston and New York, 1926. 304 pp.   205
    Primarily a study of the literary and general cultural and historical aspects of the works printed by Caxton. Treats the history of printing and of the book centers only peripherally. Supports the theory that Caxton learned printing at Cologne, basing this largely on the residence permits issued to Caxton there (see "William Caxton's Stay at Cologne," No. 197).
    "Caxton's Books in Chronological Sequence" (pp. 212-214).
    "Editions and Reprints" (pp. 215-222).
    "Caxton's Prologues, Epilogues, and Interpolations" (pp. 223-296).

BLADES, WILLIAM. *Here After Follows a Few Words on William Caxton, Merchant, Writer, and Printer, Being an Abridgment of the Biography by William Blades.* San Francisco, 1926. 20 pp.   206
    A beautifully printed condensation of Blades's biography.

BYLES, ALFRED THOMAS P., ed. *The Book of the Ordre of Chyualry. Translated and Printed by William Caxton from a French Version of Ramón Lull's "Le libre del ordre de cauayleria" together with Adam Loutfut's Scottish Transcript (Harleian MS. 6149).* London, 1926. lxviii, 143 pp. (Also for Early English Text Society. Original Series, No. 168, London, 1932.)   207
    The introduction deals with the variants between MS and book.
    "Caxton's 'Book of the ordre of chyualry or knighthode'" (p. xxii) is a description of the known copies in accordance with de Ricci's *Census* (see No. 170).
    "Caxton's Method and Style as a Translator" (pp. xlii–l) disagrees to some extent with critics of Caxton's style and use of the English language. The author feels that Caxton's close adherence to the original language is

an advantage. He includes here a fairly detailed analysis of linguistic aspects of the translations.

The top half of each page presents Caxton's translation and the bottom half the Loutfut MS text.

DOLSON, GUY BAYLEY. "Did Caxton Translate the *De consolatione philosophiae* of Boethius?" *American Journal of Philology*, 47 (1926), 83–86. 208

This brief article attempts to clarify and correct erroneous attributions of the translation of *De consolatione philosophiae* to Caxton. The author points out that Caxton, in his epilogue, clearly and unambiguously points to Chaucer as the translator.

DUFF, EDWARD GORDON. "England." *Early Illustrated Books: A History of the Declaration and Illustration of Books in the 15th and 16th Centuries*, ed. by Alfred W. Pollard. 3rd ed., London, 1926. 209

See main entry, No. 118.

COLVILLE, KENNETH NEWTON. "William Caxton: Man of Letters." *Quarterly Review*, 248 (Jan., 1927), 165–178. 210

Reviews of Plomer's *William Caxton* (No. 202) and *Wynkyn de Worde and His Contemporaries* (No. 203) and Nellie Slayton Aurner's *Caxton* (No. 205).

The reviews lead the author into a detailed evaluation of Caxton's influence on literature and language. He considers it to have been great as well as good. This is a sound and balanced estimate of Caxton's contribution to English letters and not a mere appraisal, with a basically technical approach, of his accomplishment in having introduced printing to England.

BUSHNELL, GEORGE H. "Scottish Bookbindings and Bookbinders: 1450–1800." *The Bookman's Journal*, 15 (1927), 67–87. 211

A brief general discussion followed by a "List of Scottish Bookbinders to c. 1800" which has only one binder for the 15th century.

CROTCH, WALTER JOHN BLYTH. "Caxton on the Continent." *The Library*, 4th ser., 7 (1927), 387–401. 212

A quite detailed account of the political and economic involvement of Caxton and the Mercers' Company in Continental politics, dealing particularly with their relations with the Hanseatic League. Regarding Caxton's stay at Cologne, Duff states categorically that "here Caxton learnt not only the theory but also the practice of printing, by helping with the production of Bartholomaeus's *De proprietatibus rerum* at the press of the printer of the *Flores Augustini*" (pp. 398–399).

JUCHHOFF, RUDOLF. *Drucker- und Verlegerzeichen des XV. Jahrhunderts in den Niederlanden, England, Spanien, Böhmen, und Polen*. Munich, 1927. xx, 131 pp. 213

Facsimiles and descriptions of colophons and devices.
"England" (pp. 61-72).

McMURTRIE, DOUGLAS C.   *The Golden Book. The Story of Fine
Books and Bookmaking - Past and Present.*   Chicago, 1927 (reprinted 1928; New York, 1934), 406 pp.   214
    A general history of printing. "The First Book in English" (pp. 140-
154).

PLOMER, HENRY R.   "Great Britain and Ireland." *Printing. A
Short History of the Art*, ed. by R. A. Peddie.   London, 1927,
pp. 172-209.   215
    States that Caxton "learnt the elementary part of a printer's art" in
Cologne by helping set up the Bartholomaeus. Includes a brief discussion
and description of type faces. This is a concise historical recital.

PLOMER, HENRY R.   *A Short History of English Printing, 1476-
1900.*   2nd ed., New York, 1927.   216
    See No. 135 for complete entry.

SAWYER, CHARLES J. and DARTON, F. J. HARVEY.   *Caxton to
Johnson.*   Vol. I, *English Books, 1475-1900. A Signpost for Collectors.*   Westminster [Eng.], 1927.   217
    A more-or-less popularized work for the educated layman, particularly
for the collector. Of pertinence here is only a part of Chapter III: "The
Early English Printers" (pp. 37-55).

UPDIKE, DANIEL B.   "Type and Type Forms of the Fifteenth
Century in England." *Printing Types, Their History, Forms, and
Use. A Study in Survivals.*   Cambridge [Mass.], 1927, I, 113-124.
2nd ed., 1937. 3rd ed., 1962.   218
    A detailed, illustrated study of the types of the 15th-century printers
together with historical and biographical outlines: Caxton, pp. 113-120;
Wynkyn de Worde, pp. 120-121; Notary, pp. 121-122; Lettou, p. 122; Pyn-
son, pp. 122-123; and Oxford and St. Albans, p. 123.
    Plates: Caxton, Plates 59 to 65; de Worde, Gothic types, Plate 66;
Notary and Barbier, Lettres de Forme, Plate 67; Lettou, Transitional
Gothic, Plate 68; Pynson, Lettre Batarde, Plate 69; Lettre de Forme,
Plate 70.

BOSANQUET, EUSTACE F.   "English Printed Almanacks and
Prognostications. Corrigenda and Addenda." *The Library*, 4th ser.,
8 (1928), 456-477.   219
    See No. 189.

CROTCH, WALTER JOHN BLYTH.   "Caxton Documents." *The
Library*, 4th ser., 8 (1928), 426-455.   220

A chronological listing of documents pertaining to Caxton. This is followed by reproduction of the documents in their original languages with occasional marginal translations.

CROTCH, WALTER JOHN BLYTH. *The Prologues and Epilogues of William Caxton.* Oxford, 1928. clxiii, 115 pp. (Early English Text Society. Original Series, No. 176.)   221
     Only a partial listing of the table of contents follows:
     "Documentary Summary" (pp. xv–xvii). Lists, chronologically, documentary material pertaining to Caxton.
     Bibliography (pp. xix–xxiv).
     "Biographical Introduction" (pp. xxvii–cxxv). The lengthy introduction sets off Caxton against his period, not only as a printer, but also as merchant, diplomat, and translator.
     "Additional Notes. Caxton's Daughter, Colard Mansion" (pp. cxxvii–cxxxi).
     Appendix (pp. cxxxiii–clxiii).
     The prologues and epilogues are printed with the same line arrangement as that used by Caxton and are arranged chronologically.
     The "Biographical Introduction" noted above is the best life of Caxton up to the present.

OSWALD, JOHN CLYDE. "William Caxton and His Contemporaries," *A History of Printing. Its Development through Five Hundred Years.* New York and London, 1928. pp. 190–207.   222
     A brief, rather cursory discussion of no particular significance other than as a historical account.

OWST, GERALD ROBERT. "Books and Book-Owners of 15th Century St. Albans." *St. Albans Architectural Society. Transactions* (1928), pp. 176–195.   223
     Not examined.

THOMAS, HENRY. *The Beginning of Printing in London. Souvenir of the Lord Mayor's Show.* London, 1928. 10 pp.   224
     Souvenir pamphlet of no particular value. A brief summary of the introduction of printing to England, stressing specifically London printers.

THOMAS, HENRY. *Wilh. Caxton uyss Engelant. Evidence that the First English Printer Learned His Craft at Cologne.* Cologne, 1928. 14 pp.   225
     On the basis of evidence "not available to Blades" asserts that Caxton learned printing in Cologne. Bases his entire argument on the eighth stanza of the poem Wynkyn de Worde printed in his 1495 edition of *De proprietatibus rerum.*

BIRCH, J. G.   "Caxton and His Craft." *The Connoisseur: A Magazine for Collectors*, 84 (1929), 297.   226
A brief account of Birch's discovery of Caxton's residence permits in Cologne. The pertinent entries are reproduced. (See also No. 197).

BULLEN, HENRY LEWIS. "New Light on William Caxton." *Inland Printer*, 82, No. 1 (1929), 95–96.   227
A brief review of Caxton finds, devoted primarily to the discovery of the indulgences of 1476.

BURGER, C. P.   "Een Engelsch perkamentboekje uit den incunabeltijd: 'The Primer on Vellum Printed by Wm. de Machlinia about 1484.'" *Het Boek*, 18 (1929), 203–205.   228
Though basically a book review of George Smith's work (see No. 235), this entry is of interest because it presents a summary of the scholarship on this topic.

CROTCH, WALTER JOHN BLYTH.   "Caxton's Son-in-Law." *The Library*, 4th ser., 9 (1929), 48–52.   229
Traces and describes the litigation, financial difficulties, and ultimate divorce of Caxton's daughter, Elizabeth, from her husband, Gerard Crop. Includes transcriptions of pertinent documents.
In this same volume are letters (pp. 325–326) pertaining to this article.

GREG, WALTER W.   "MS Source of Caxton's Second Edition of the *Canterbury Tales*." *Publications of the Modern Language Association*, 44 (1929), 1251–1253.   230
A brief critique of, together with some objections to, Miss Kilgour's article on Caxton's MS source (see No. 234). A brief rejoinder from Miss Kilgour follows.

HOBSON, GEOFFREY D. *Bindings in Cambridge Libraries ... Based on Researches by N. F. Burwell, H. M. Davies and the late Charles E. Sayle.* Cambridge [Eng.], 1929. xvi, 179 pp., 72 plates.
231
Detailed descriptions and discussions of bindings, including eight 15th-century English bindings. Remarks on the binder and history of each volume are included. Well illustrated.

HOBSON, GEOFFREY D. *English Binding Before 1500.* Cambridge [Eng.], 1929. 58 pp. (The Sandars Lectures for 1927).   232
A brief historical account of the period. Discusses and describes blind stamps. Of pertinence and interest are also the following appendices:
Appendix G: "An Attempted Classification of Oxford 15th Century Bindings" (pp. 48–49).
Appendix H: "English Cut Leatherwork, 1300–1500" (pp. 50–52).

Appendix J: "Additional 15th Century English Bindings and a List of English 'small stamp' Binderies Working Before 1510" (pp. 53–55).

ISAAC, FRANK. "Types Used by Wynkyn de Worde, 1501–1534." *The Library*, 4th ser., 9 (1929), 395–410. 233

Lists and describes types used by Wynkyn de Worde and gives list of works in which they were used. With facsimiles.

KILGOUR, MARGARET. "The Manuscript Source of Caxton's Second Edition of the *Canterbury Tales*." *Publications of the Modern Language Association*, 44 (1929), 186–201. 234

This study is a further attempt to confirm the source of Caxton's second edition and had its impetus in the earlier work on the subject by Greg (see No. 198). Miss Kilgour uses Greg's method of close collation and comparison of a section of the text, in this case the "Pardoner's Tale."

The variants in MSS are listed in tabular form. The author concludes that the MS labeled A3 (BM Addit. 35286) is the most likely source for Caxton's second printing.

See Greg's critique of this article in the same volume on pp. 1251–1253.

SMITH, GEORGE. *William de Machlinia: The Primer on Vellum Printed by Him in London About 1484. Newly Found and Described.* London, 1929. 26 pp. 235

General brief history of primers, including their typographical background, pp. 7–14. Description of Machlinia's *Primer*, pp. 14–17. Brief biography of Machlinia, pp. 17–23. The remainder of the little volume is devoted to facsimiles of the woodcuts.

PLOMER, HENRY R. "The Importation of Low Country and French Books into England, 1480 and 1502–03." *The Library*, 4th ser., 9 (1929), 164–168. 236

A brief article expanding on the author's earlier one dealing with the English book trade (see No. 201).

POLLARD, ALFRED W. "The New Caxton Indulgence." *The Library*, 4th ser., 9 (1929), 86–89. 237

A description and transcription of the indulgence issued by the Abbot of Abingdon and printed largely in Caxton's type 2. See also *The Times* (London), Feb. 7, 1928.

BYLES, ALFRED T. P. "Caxton's *Book of the Ordre of Chyualry*: A French Manuscript in Brussels." *Review of English Studies*, 6 (1930), 305–308. 238

A detailed description of a French MS of *L'ordre de chevalerie*, which the author discovered in the Bibliothèque Royale in Brussels. Gives a history of the MS, but does not establish a direct connection between it and

Caxton except that "it was from some MS of this type that Caxton made his translation."

CROTCH, WALTER JOHN BLYTH. "William Caxton: An Englishman of the Fifteenth Century." *Economica; A Journal of the Social Sciences,* 10 (1930), 56–73.   239
  A brief biography stressing Caxton's mercantile activities. Also includes a detailed discussion of the economic and political influence of the Company of the Mercers.

HITTMAIR, RUDOLF. "Aus der Frühzeit des englischen Buchdruckes." *Verhandlungen der 57. Versammlung deutscher Philologen und Schulmänner* (1930), p. 101.   240
  A brief summary of a paper read at a conference. A routine recital of the basic historical and biographical facts of Caxton's beginnings as printer and publisher.

MAURER, F. "William Caxton, geb. etwa 1412." *Graphische Revue,* 33 (1930), 231, 237.   241
  Not examined.

ROBERTS, W. WRIGHT. "William Caxton, Writer and Critic." *The John Rylands Library. Bulletin,* 14 (1930), 410–422.   242
  Examines the one important facet of Caxton frequently relegated to a minor role in the major biographical studies (e.g. Blades and Duff), namely Caxton's contribution to the literary and cultural climate of 15th-century England. The author regards Caxton as an integral yet superior influence in his era. He also discusses Caxton's literary style. A sympathetic, scholarly contribution.

STEIN, ELIZABETH. "Caxton's *Recuyell* and Shakespeare's *Troilus.*" *Modern Language Notes,* 45 (1930), 144–146.   243
  A brief note on literary sources. Establishes that in Act IV of *Troilus* Shakespeare used material not in Lydgate's *Troy Book* but in Caxton's *Recuyell.*

WIENCKE, H. *Die Sprache Caxtons.* Cologne, 1930. 226 pp. (Kölner anglistische Arbeiten, 11.)   244
  Not examined.

ELLIS, F. S., ed. *The Golden Legend or Lives of the Saints as Englished by Wm. Caxton.* London, 1931.   245
  A printing of the work with no editorial comment.

HARE, WILLIAM LOFTUS. "A Newly Discovered Volume Printed by William Caxton, 'Pylgremage of the Sowle.'" *Apollo: A Journal of the Arts,* 14, No. 82 (1931), 205–213.   246

Also published the same year in London under the title *John Lydgate's* *"Pylgremage of the Sowle."* *Printed by William Caxton at Westminster, June 6th, 1483; a Hitherto Unknown Copy.*

This is the first detailed account of the volume after its discovery.

Part I contains biographical information and Part II literary history. Four pages of facsimiles and illustrations are included.

HITTMAIR, RUDOLF. *Caxton, Englands erster Drucker und Verleger.* Innsbruck, 1931. 53 pp.   247

A general biography and evaluation of Caxton. Hittmair is convinced that Caxton learned printing at Cologne. He credits Caxton with recognizing and, through the language he uses in his books, with spreading and perpetuating the linguistic movement emanating from London, thus helping to establish a universal tongue in England.

BONE, GAVIN. "Extant Manuscripts Printed by W. de Worde with Notes on the Owner, Roger Thorney." *The Library*, 4th ser., 12 (1932), 284–306.   248

An attempt, based on careful examination of the MSS and some collation of the printed and written texts, to determine the exact MS source for some 15th-century English printed books.

The major work discussed is Lydgate's *Siege of Thebes*, printed by Wynkyn de Worde. Through comparison with the printed text Bone notes and describes certain marks on the St. Johns College MS which are clearly printers' marks. He follows the same procedure for de Worde's *Assembly of Gods* (c. 1498) and finds that the marks on the Trinity College MS match the printed version.

Also included is a brief biography of Roger Thorney, a mercer, who had owned the MSS and acted as patron of the press.

BYLES, ALFRED THOMAS P., ed. *The Book of Fayttes of Armes and of Chyualry. Translated and Printed by William Caxton; from the French Original by Christine de Pisan.* Oxford, 1932. lvi, 315 pp. (Early English Text Society. Original Series, No. 189.) 249

The introduction (pp. xi–lvi), aside from literary and source discussions, contains the following sections which are specifically pertinent:

III. "The Printers" (pp. xxvi–xxxvi). Byles dates Caxton's printing as 1490, thus following Blades rather than other authorities. Includes a description of the Caxton book and of extant copies.

V. "The Translator" (pp. li–lv). Considers Caxton's style better and on firmer footing here than in earlier works. He notes an extremely close adherence to the original French version. Comments also on frequent intrusions of tautological word pairings and other French influences.

JUCHHOFF, RUDOLF, ed. *Dialogus de libertate ecclesiastica. London. John Lettou und Wilhelmus de Machlinia um 1483.* Lichtdruckwiedergabe der Berliner Bruchstücke mit einer Einleitung. Berlin, 1932. 14 pp., facsim. 4 pp.   250

This fragment is the only extant part of this imprint. The entire fragment is reproduced. It was discovered as the end paper in a copy of Johannes Jacobus Bergomensis' *Supplementum chronicarum* (1485). The editor's introduction traces the history of the printing as well as of the contents of the work and assigns it to the shop of Lettou and Machlinia on the basis of the type design.

McKERROW, RONALD B. and FERGUSON, FREDERIC S. *Title-Page Borders Used in England and Scotland, 1485–1640*. London, 1932 [for 1931]. xlvii, 234 pp. (Bibliographical Society. Illustrated Monographs, No. 21.)   251
Only a few 15th-century title-page borders are included in this volume, which gives only those "cut either on a single piece of wood or metal, or on pieces evidently intended to form part of a single design."
Items 1–9 and 11 were used by Machlinia, Pynson, Wynkyn de Worde, and Notary, but, with the exception of items 1 and 2, only in their 16th-century imprints.

GESSLER, JEAN. *Fragment d'anciens traités pour l'enseignement du Français en Angleterre*. New York, 1933. 21 pp. (Publication of the Institute of French Studies, Inc., Columbia University.) 252
Establishes the edition of: 1, a fragment of Caxton's *Dialogues* (Oxford, Bodleian, Douce, *d.* 2); and 2, Wynkyn de Worde's Bodleian, Douce, f. 2. Ascribes Badfords Ballads, I. C. 40, fd. 21, to Pynson.

LATHROP, HENRY B. *Translations from the Classics into English from Caxton to Chapman, 1477–1620*. Madison, 1933. (University of Wisconsin Studies in Language and Literature, No. 35).   253
Pertinent to this listing is Chapter I only: "The Age of Caxton, 1477–1517" (pp. 15–28). This is primarily an examination of the works themselves rather than of their translators, but the author does make a brief complimentary reference, though obliquely, to Caxton's style.

SUSEBACH, HEINZ, ed. *Caxton: Tulle of Olde Age. Textuntersuchung mit literarischer Einführung*. Halle, 1933. xxii, 118 pp. (Studien zur englischen Philologie, No. 75).   254
A reprint of *Tulle of Olde Age* with a brief introduction. The author states that Caxton learned printing at Cologne, but that the *Recuyell* was printed in Bruges (p. x). The main part of the introduction (pp. ix–xxii) deals with textual and MS comparison and analysis.

WINKLER, GERDA. *Das Relativum bei Caxton und seine Entwicklung von Chaucer bis Spenser*. Saalfeld, [1933]. iii, 82 pp.   255
A doctoral dissertation not examined.

CLARK, JOHN W. "A New Copy of Caxton's Indulgence." *Speculum*, 9 (1934), 301–303.   256

A detailed description of a copy of the first issue of Caxton's 1481 indulgence. A transcription of the text, 80 percent complete, is appended.

HITTMAIR, RUDOLF. *Aus Caxtons Vorreden und Nachreden.*
Vol. I, *Aus Schrifttum und Sprache der Angelsachsen.* Leipzig,
1934. 257
A detailed examination of the prefaces and epilogues for the *Recuyell*, *Jason*, and *Eneydos*. The author selected these because they represent both the beginning and the end of Caxton's period of activity as printer and translator, are based on classical themes, are from French sources, and are essentially entertainment literature. Following each pertinent prologue and epilogue, its literary, linguistic, and historical aspects are examined.

THOMAS, HENRY. "An Indulgence Printed by Pynson, 1491."
British Museum Quarterly, 9 (1934), 32–33. 258
The date of imprint of this indulgence is thought to antedate Pynson's first printed book. The copy under discussion is the only one known with this imprint.

ADAM, LEONHARD. "Oxford und Cambridge und ihre Universi-
tätsdruckereien." *Deutsche Rundschau*, 245 (Oct. 1935),
33–44. 259
A general discussion of the university presses at Oxford and Cambridge. Only a very brief reference (p. 41) to 15th-century printing at Oxford.

BROADUS, EDMUND KEMPER. "Simple Person (Caxton)." *Satur-
day and Sunday*. Toronto, 1935. pp. 87–98. 260
Originally published in *The University Magazine* (April 1913) under the title "William Caxton: Simple Person."
The author stresses the high moral and idealistic tendencies of Caxton. He attempts to understand the man as a human being rather than as an innovator or successful merchant.

BÜHLER, CURT F. "The Dictes and Sayings of the Philosophers." *The Library*, 4th ser., 15 (1935), 316–329. 261
Establishes that the third edition (1489) of *The Dictes* was reset from the first edition (1477). Expresses some doubts on Blades's chronological order of Caxtons. Feels that types 2 and 2* were in use at the same time, with the latter used as early as 1477. In a postscript R. B. McK(errow) agrees with Bühler on the basis of typographical comparison of the three editions.

BYLES, ALFRED T. P. "William Caxton as a Man of Letters."
The Library, 4th ser., 15 (1935), 1–25. 262
This is a study of Caxton's style and an evaluation of his status as a man of letters. The author points out the frequent intrusions of French idiom and syntax in Caxton's translations as well as his not infrequent

awkward constructions, but he places Caxton in the literary and cultural
mainstream of his period.

DAVIES, HUGH WILLIAMS. *Devices of the Early Printers, 1457–
1560. Their History and Development.* London, 1935.   263
   A general work on the subject. Reproductions with explanatory notes.
The arrangement of the reproductions can be confusing as it follows
heraldic rules rather than bibliographic or biographic logic.
   Caxton: fig. 197; Wynkyn de Worde: figs. 56, 197–199; Richard Pynson:
figs. 19, 70.

HODNETT, EDWARD. *English Woodcuts, 1480–1535.* London,
1935 [for 1934]. xv, 483 pp. (The Bibliographical Society. Illustrated Monographs, No. 22.)   264
   The first group of numbers after the name of a printer or printers in the
list below refers to the introduction, which, under the printer's name, presents a discussion of his use of woodcuts. The second group of numbers
refers to the pertinent pages in "Bibliography of Illustrated Books, 1480–
1535." This too is divided chronologically by printers. The third group
of numbers refers to the specific printer in the "Catalogue of Cuts in
English Printed Books, 1480–1535." This is a descriptive, numbered listing of the individual cuts. The numbers after "figs." lists the illustrations.
   William Caxton: 1–7, 75–76, 111–163, figs. 1–21.
   Wynkyn de Worde: 7–32, 76–93, 164–317, figs. 22–115.
   Richard Pynson: 32–46, 93–99, 318–392, figs. 116–172.
   William de Machlinia: 47, 102, 407, fig. 196.
   Theodoric Rood and Thomas Hunter: 47–48, 105, 441–443, figs. 173,
175, 178.
   St. Albans Schoolmaster: 48, 106, 446–447, fig. 228.
   Julian Notary, John Barbier, and I. H. (Jean Huvin?): 48–53, 102–103,
408–432, figs. 179–182, 205, 210–215.

LUCAS, FRANK L. " 'Honest Ovid Among the Goths,' " *Authors
Dead and Living.* New York, 1935. pp. 39–45.   265
   An urbane, witty, whimsical, and erudite discussion of the extant parts
of Caxton's translation of the *Metamorphoses* (Books X–XV). The author
compares Caxton's translation with the original from a literary and linguistic standpoint and deals with Caxton as a cultural influence, rather than as
a printer.

OAKESHOTT, WALTER F. "Caxton and Malory's *Morte Darthur.*"
Gutenberg Jahrbuch (1935), pp. 112–116.   266
   The main emphasis in this brief article is on Caxton's rewriting and re-
vision of Malory's text.

PIRCKHOFER, ANTON. "Zum syntaktischen Gebrauch des

bestimmten Artikels bei Caxton." *Englische Studien*, 70, No. 1
(1935), 92-101. 267
    A detailed morphological examination of Caxton's use of the definite
article. Comparisons are also made with the translations of the Earl
Rivers to determine the uniformity of printers' language during the 15th
century.

DODGSON, CAMBELL. *English Woodcuts of the 15th Century*.
Strassburg, 1936., 10 pp. 23 reproductions. 268
    Not examined.

MATTHES, HEINRICH CHRISTOPH. "Caxton-Miszellen." *Archiv
für das Studium der neueren Sprachen und Literatur*, 169 (1936), 228-
229. 269
    Has a brief reference to orthographic differences between the first
200 pages and the remainder of Caxton's *Recuyell* and a one-sentence reference to the possibility that the *Eneydos* translation was printed after
Caxton's death (cf. No. 257, Hittmair, *Aus Caxtons Vorreden und Nachreden*).

POLLARD, ALFRED W., ed. *Le morte Darthur. The Story of King
Arthur and of His Noble Knights of the Round Table, Written by Sir
Thomas Malory, First Printed by William Caxton, Now Modernised
as to Spelling and Punctuation*. 3 vols. London, New York, 1936.
270
    The discussion of the literary and printing history of the work is brief
(pp. vii–x). Includes "Preface of William Caxton" (pp. xi–xv).

BOSANQUET, EUSTACE F. [Letter to editor of *The Library*].
The Library, 4th ser., 17 (1937), 362-363. 271
    A response to Part III of "Three Notes on Caxton" by C. F. Bühler in
the same volume (pp. 163–166). Bosanquet disagrees with Bühler. (See
No. 273 for details).

BÜHLER, CURT F. "Caxton Variants." *The Library*, 4th ser.,
17 (1937), 62-69. 272
    By comparing different copies of the same book, Bühler proves that, in
case of an error discovered after a quire had come off the press, corrections were made during a run. The following are examined (with pertinent
facsimiles): *Game and Playe of the Chesse* (pp. 63–65), *The Book Callid
Caton* (pp. 65–67), and *Boke of Eneydos* (pp. 67–68).

BÜHLER, CURT F. "Three Notes on Caxton." *The Library*, 4th
ser., 17 (1937), 155-166. 273
    A discussion of several of the Caxton half-sheets found by Blades in a
binding of *Boethius*.
    Part I is concerned primarily with the dating of Caxton's types 2 and 2*
(see *The Library*, 4th ser., 15[1935], 316–329). The author believes that

types 2 and 2* "were in use at the same time and that the latter was employed as early as 1477."

In Part II Bühler disagrees with Blades's statement that the *Book callid
Caton* was printed with types 2 and 4* and follows Duff and the *Gesamtkatalog* in holding that the types are 2* and 4*.

Part III proposes that the sheets of Lydgate's *Lyf of our Lady* discovered by Blades are printer's waste of an edition that has disappeared
rather than canceled sheets. Bosanquet disagrees with this theory in a
letter to the editor (see No. 271).

BYLES, ALFRED THOMAS P., ed. *The Book of the Fayttes of
Armes and of Chyualry. Translated and Printed by William Caxton;
from the French Original by Christine de Pisan.* Rev. ed., with
corrections. Oxford, 1937. lvi, 315 pp. (Early English Text So-
ciety. Original Series, No. 189.)   274
    See No. 249 full entry.

HAMMERSCHLAG, JOHANNES. *Dialekteinflüsse im frühenglis-
chen Wortschatz, nachgewiesen an Caxton und Fabyan.* Bonn, 1937.
142 pp. (Bonner Studien zur englischen Philologie, Heft 31.)   275
    Shows the dialect influences in early modern English, using primarily
the works of Caxton and Fabyan. This exclusively philological study is a
very detailed and scholarly work which also serves to indicate Caxton's
great influence on the written language of his own and subsequent periods.
    "Das Wortmaterial bei Caxton und Fabyan" (pp. 49–113) is the main part
of the pertinent material. Detailed source references are provided for each
work examined.
    "Liste der untersuchten Wörter" (p. 123).
    Bibliography (pp. 125–126).
    Sources (MSS and early printed books) are given on pp. 127–140.

HIGGINS, FRANCIS. "William Caxton, Printer." *St. Nicholas,*
64 (May, 1937), 54–55.   276
    Not examined.

WINSHIP, GEORGE PARKER. *William Caxton and His Work. A
Paper Read at a Meeting of the Club of Odd Volumes in Boston,
Massachusetts, in January 1908; With a Letter from the Author.*
Berkeley, 1937. xi, 55 pp.   277
    Except for a summary rehearsal of known facts about Caxton, this is a
work of largely baseless speculation, the main theme of which is that Cax-
ton was not a printer.

BÜHLER, CURT F. "Libri impressi cum notis manuscriptis."
Modern Language Notes, 53 (1938), 245–249.   278
    Proposes to examine marginal notations of literary value in early
printed books. Not directly pertinent, but does discuss notes in a Caxton
work (Boethius' *De consolatione philosophiae*).

BÜHLER, CURT F. "Notes on a Pynson Volume." *The Library*, 4th ser., 18 (1938), 261-267. 279
An attempt to date *Old Tenures*, printed by Pynson. Beale dated it 1504, but Bühler, largely on the basis of typographical examination and comparison, assigns it to 1494.

HART, JAMES D., ed. *Original Leaf from the First Edition of Alexander Barclay's English Translation of Sebastian Brant's "Ship of Fools," Printed by Richard Pynson in 1509; With an Essay*. San Francisco, 1938. 280
Not examined.

JACKSON, HOLBROOK. "William Caxton," *Printing of Books*. London, 1938. pp. 186-195. 281
A brief essay on Caxton containing a biographical, technical, literary, and historical evaluation.

POLLARD, GRAHAM. "The Company of Stationers Before 1557." *The Library*, 4th ser., 18 (1938), 1-38. 282
A detailed account, well documented, tracing the history, organization, function, and importance in the book trade of the Company of Stationers.

POLLARD, GRAHAM. "Lettou's Address; A Correction." *The Library*, 4th ser., 18 (1938), 335-337. 283
This brief article is a correction of a statement referring to Lettou's address in the author's earlier "The Company of Stationers Before 1557," *The Library* (1938), p. 21.

WINSHIP, GEORGE PARKER. *William Caxton and the First English Press. A Bio-bibliographical Essay*. New York, 1938. xi, 44 pp. 284
A biography with general historical and cultural background of the 15th century. Also discusses Caxton's more important works in some detail.

GLENISTER, SIDNEY H. "Gutenberg and Caxton, Pioneers of Printing," *Stories of Great Craftsmen*. Toronto, 1939. pp. 13-27. 285
Not examined.

LAW, F. H. "Gutenberg, Manutius and Caxton, the First Great Printers," *Civilization Builders*. New York, 1939. pp. 116-122. 286
A very brief, popularized essay intended for the teen-age reader.

PLANT, MARJORIE. *The English Book Trade. An Economic History of the Making and Sale of Books*. London, 1939. 500 pp. 287

Contains little material pertinent to the period before 1501 since the trade was then still in its infancy. The work is by an economic historian.

POVEY, KENNETH. "The Caxton Indulgence of 1476." *The Library*, 4th ser., 19 (1939), 462–464.   288
    A reprinted composite of the indulgence based on two MS versions discovered in the library of Queen's University, Belfast. Caxton's printing was published by A. W. Pollard (*The Library*, 4th ser., 9 [1929], 86–89).

VINAVER, EUGÈNE. "A Note on the Earliest Printed Text of Malory's *Morte d'Arthur.*" *John Rylands Library. Bulletin*, 23 (1939), 102–106.   289
    Presents a theory to explain the existence of the variants in the two extant copies of Caxton's printing of the *Morte d'Arthur*, the one in the J. Pierpont Morgan Library, the other in the John Rylands Library. These major variants are folios 308 recto and verso, 311 recto and verso, 330 recto and verso, and 383 recto and verso. For a reply see C. F. Bühler, "Two Caxton Problems," *The Library*, 4th ser., 20 (1940), 266–271 (entry No. 293).

BÜHLER, CURT F. "A Bibliographical Curiosity." *Bibliographical Society of America. Papers*, 35 (1940), 58–60.   290
    Examines the manner in which the reading *fecii* (instead of *fecit*) appears to have crept into standard bibliographies of early English books from Caxton's *Doctrinal of Sapience*. The author believes it to be based on faulty reading of a facsimile and stresses the necessity of referring to original copies, and more than one, if possible.

BÜHLER, CURT F. "Caxton's *History of Jason.*" *Bibliographical Society of America. Papers*, 34 (1940), 254–261.   291
    Points out the differences in the *History of Jason* as found in copies in the Nationalbibliothek (Vienna), the New York Public Library, the J. Pierpont Morgan Library, the John Rylands Library, and the British Museum. He finds that the British Museum copy is partially "restored" and thus not reliable.

BÜHLER, CURT F. "Caxton Studies." *Gutenberg Jahrbuch* (1940), pp. 169–176.   292
    The first section of the paper deals with the quality of Caxton's type. On the basis of close examination of a fragment of the *Fayettes of Armes and of Chyualrye* Bühler concludes that Caxton's type was well cut, but that the quality of the ink was poor.
    The second section discusses how this fragment came to be printed and bound with a different run.
    The third section briefly seeks to account for displaced type in one of the Morgan Library copies of the *Book callid Caton* (PML 691).

BÜHLER, CURT F. "Two Caxton Problems." *The Library*, 4th ser., 20 (1940), 266–271.   293

Part I is a reply to Eugène Vinaver's "A Note on the Earliest Printed Text of Malory's *Morte d'Arthur*," *John Rylands Library Bulletin*, 23 (1939), 102–106. Vinaver believes *Morte Darthur* was printed in quarto, but Blades, de Ricci, and Bühler agree that it is a folio. Bühler's view is based on an examination of the Morgan Library copy. The text on leaves 308, 311, 380, and 385 of the Morgan and Rylands copies are of different type settings. Bühler supposes the printers ran off too few copies of these sheets.

Part II is a reply to Bosanquet's letter (see No. 271). Bühler presents further evidence to support his theory expressed in Part III of "Three Notes on Caxton" (pp. 163–166) in the above volume.

KINGERY, ROBERT E. "Anonymous Printer of St. Albans," Part 3. *Hobbies, the Magazine for Collectors*, 45 (March, 1940), 94.   294

A brief discussion of the type fonts used by the Printer of St. Albans. His mark is also reproduced.

Parts 1 and 2 were not available for examination.

LEHMANN-HAUPT, HELLMUT. "Englische Holzstempelalphabete des 15. Jahrhunderts." *Gutenberg Jahrbuch* (1940), pp. 93-97.   295

Deals with clay tiles stamped with wooden alphabet stamps. Has only peripheral pertinence here.

M. M. "Pynson's Book of Hours." *More Books. The Bulletin of the Boston Public Library*, 15 (1940), 380.   296

A copy of the *Horea beate marie virginis*, printed by Pynson in 1514 and acquired by the Boston Public Library, is briefly described.

WINSHIP, GEORGE PARKER. *Printing in the Fifteenth Century.* Philadelphia, 1940. London, 1941. xi, 158 pp. (The A. S. W. Rosenwald Fellowship in Bibliography, Publications No. 7.)   297

The main stress of this volume is on Continental printing. English printing, as centered around Caxton, is discussed briefly (pp. 143–158). Lack of an index is a great defect.

BÜHLER, CURT F. "English Incunabula in America." *The Library Quarterly*, 11 (1941), 497-501.   298

A brief article indicating the number of English imprints in American libraries.

BÜHLER, CURT F. "*The Churl and the Bird* and *The Dictes and Sayings of the Philosophers*: Two Notes." *The Library*, 4th ser., 21 (1941), 279-290.   299

Part I: "The Two Caxton Editions of *The Churl and the Bird*" (pp. 279–284). Blades, Sayles, de Ricci, Duff, and the *STC* state that the Cambridge University Library copy of this work is the first and the Morgan

Library copy the second edition. After close comparison of the texts Bühler finds the reverse to be true. The Morgan copy agrees with nearly all earlier MSS, whereas the Cambridge copy does not. The author contends further that the second edition is probably a reprint of the first and that the same MS was used for both.

Part II: "More About *The Dictes and Sayings of the Philosophers*" (pp. 284–290). This is an attempt to establish the proper sequence for the two editions of *The Dictes* and to account for some variants in the two extant copies.

GESSLER, JEAN. *Deux manuels de conversation imprimés en Angleterre au XVe siècle.* Brussels, 1941.   300
  Not examined.

WORKMAN, SAMUEL K. "Versions by Skelton, Caxton, and Berners of a Prologue by Diodorus Siculus." *Modern Language Notes,* 16 (1941), 252–258.   301
  Establishes that the first three-fourths of the prologue to the *Polycronicon* was translated by Caxton from the preface to the *Library of History* by Diodorus Siculus. The main part of the brief article then compares the three versions noted in the title. Largely of interest to the student of stylistics.

DISRAELI, ISAAC. *A Trilogy on Printing History.* 3 vols. Cincinnati, 1942. (Selections reprinted from his *Amenities of Literature*; Foreword by Lloyd Emerson Siberell.)   302
  Vol. I: *Invention of Printing.*
  Vol. II: *Part I, The First English Printer. Part II, Early Libraries.*
  Vol. III: *The War Against Books.*
  All three of these small volumes contain material pertaining to 15th-century English printing, particularly Vol. II, Part I, which deals with Caxton. Says Caxton learned printing in Cologne and also printed his translation of the *Recuyell* there. Disraeli does not esteem Caxton's contribution to literature and culture very highly. Shows little understanding of Caxton's unique contribution to English cultural life beyond the purely technical aspects. The collection is of interest primarily because of the author rather than as a contribution to scholarship.

SCHULZ, H. C. "Manuscript Printer's Copy for a Lost Early English Book." *The Library,* 4th ser., 22 (1942), 138–144.   303
  Manuscript HM 130 in the Huntington Library, *The Prick of Conscience,* formerly attributed to Richard Rolle, is a marked printer's copy. The MS is described and there is some conjecture by the author as to the identity of the printer (Wynkyn de Worde?) no printed copy having survived.

WILLIAMS, E. HARCOURT. *William Caxton. A Story Play for Young Players.* London, 1942. 27 pp. (French's Plays for Juvenile Performers, No. 50.)   304

A pleasant one-act play. Caxton is imbued with a bit more virtue and insight than he probably possessed, but this piece is, after all, for the moral uplift of children.

BENNETT, HENRY STANLEY. "Caxton and His Public." *Review of English Studies*, 19 (1943), 113–119.   305
   Refers to an article by Lathrop (see No. 195) dealing with Caxton's influence on the contemporary reader. Gives Caxton no credit for setting literary taste or for influencing English literature because he "had only to reap where others had sown."

BÜHLER, CURT F. "Variants in English Incunabula." *Bookmen's Holiday. Notes and Studies Written and Gathered in Tribute to Harry Lydenberg*. New York, 1943. pp. 459–474.   306
   Part I deals with the general topic, treating primarily the causes for variants. The author considers the latter due mainly to either technical causes (e.g. errors of imposition or composition) or accidental causes (e.g. imperfection left uncorrected, imperfection corrected by reset type, or incorrect number of leaves or quires printed).
   Part II uses three variants to illustrate these causes. The examples are Pynson's edition of the *Canterbury Tales* (c. 1491), the Oxford 1482 imprint of Lathbury's *Liber moralium super threnis Jeremiae* and the Wynkyn de Worde printing of Lyndewode's *Constitutiones provinciales* of 1496.

McMURTRIE, DOUGLAS C. *The Book. The Story of Printing and Bookmaking*. New York, 1943.   307
   See No. 214.

BÜHLER, CURT F. "The Binding of Books Printed by William Caxton." *Bibliographical Society of America. Papers*, 38 (1944), 1–8.   308
   Disagrees with Blades's contention (in *The Life and Typography of William Caxton* [London, 1861–1863], II, lviii) that Caxton had his books bound immediately after printing. Presents evidence that only a few copies were "bound for immediate sale or display and that the remaining sheets were stored until such time as they were needed."

HOBSON, GEOFFREY D. *Blind-stamped Panels in the English Book-Trade, c. 1485–1555*. London, 1944. 111 pp. (The Bibliographical Society. Supplement to *Transactions*, No. 17.)   309
   Theorizes that the first stamped bindings were brought to England by Machlinia. Discusses Continental bindings as well as English ones that entered the English book market (pp. 10–29).

JACOB, ERNEST FRASER. "*The Book of St. Albans*." *The John Rylands Library. Bulletin*, 28 (1944), 99–118.   310
   A lecture delivered in the John Rylands Library on March 10, 1943. This

is a discussion of the *Book of St. Albans* stressing the content and its relation to its period. The author ascribes only the *Book of Hunting and Fishing* to Dame Juliana Berners and not the *Liber armorum*, which is earlier.
Does not deal with the printing history except incidentally.

BÜHLER, CURT F. "Caxton's *Blanchardin and Eglantine*: Notes
on the Leaf Preserved in the British Museum." *Bibliographical
Society of America. Papers*, 39 (1945), 156–161.   311
    Considers the sheet in question as being a cancel. Bases this on a
comparison with the EETS edition of *Blanchardin and Eglantine*, which
uses the John Rylands Library copy.

CANDLIN, E. FRANK. "William Caxton of Bruge: First English
Printer." *Message; Belgian Review*, 39 (May 1945), 43–45.   312
    A popularized recital of Caxton's learning to print from Mansion.
Recognizes Caxton's cultural as well as his technical and mercantile
achievements.

ORCUTT, WILLIAM DANA. "William Caxton Establishes the English Language," *From My Library Walls; A Kaleidoscope of Memor-
ies*. New York, Toronto, 1945. pp. 121–124.   313
    A brief biography of Caxton in reminiscences of a bibliophile and bibli-
ographer.

JOHNSON, JOHN DE MONIUS and GIBSON, STRICKLAND. *Print
and Privilege at Oxford to the Year 1700*. Oxford, 1946. (Oxford
Bibliographical Society, Vol. VII.)   314
    Has very slight material on the incunabula period since the Chancellor's
Registers covering the two early periods of printing (1478–1486 and 1517–
1519) are lost.

MARY JEREMY, SISTER. "Caxton's *Golden Legend* and Vara-
gine's *Legenda aurea*." *Speculum*, 21 (1946), 212–221.   315
    A study that examines Caxton's abilities as a translator from Latin by
comparing his English edition with the Latin of Voragine. The article is of
interest to the philologist and literary scholar.

PAFORT, ELOISE. "A Group of Early Tudor School-Books." *The
Library*, 4th ser., 26 (1946), 227–261.   316
    Though several of the books included were printed first in the 16th cen-
tury, this article is nevertheless pertinent here because several of the
printers began their efforts in the 15th century.
    Under each title there is a description of the various editions. This is
followed by a list of editions and the printers. Only the English printers
are listed below.
    1. John Stanbridge, *Parvula*; editions by Rood, Wynkyn de Worde, and
Pynson (pp. 228–233).

2. John Stanbridge, *Vulgaria*; editions by de Worde (pp. 233-236).

3. *Os, facies, mentum*; editions by de Worde (pp. 236-237).

4. John Stanbridge, *Sum, es, fui* and *Gradus comparationum*; editions by de Worde and Pynson (pp. 237-242).

5. Robert Whittinton, *De heteroclitis nominibus*; editions by de Worde, Notary, and Pynson (pp. 242-245).

6. Robert Whittinton, *Lucubrationes*; editions by Pynson and de Worde (pp. 245-249).

7. Robert Whittinton, *De nominum generibus*; editions by Pynson and de Worde (pp. 249-254).

8. Cicero, *The Three Bookes of Tullyes Offyces*; editions by de Worde (pp. 254-255).

9. *Expositio hymnorum* and *Expositio sequentiorum*; editions by Pynson, Notary, and de Worde (pp. 255-260).

10. Murmellius, *Composita verborum*; editions by de Worde (pp. 260-261).

HOUSMAN, JOHN E.   "Higden, Trevisa, Caxton and the Beginnings of Arthurian Criticism." *Review of English Studies*, 23 (1947), 209-217.   317
Section IV (pp. 214-217) discusses Caxton's view that historical invention is more important than merely literary invention. Cites Caxton on this, especially in relation to didactic and moral aspects of historical personages.

LEISI, ERNST. *Die tautologischen Wortpaare in Caxtons "Eneydos." Zur synchronischen Bedeutungs- und Ursachenforschung.* Cambridge [Mass.], 1947. 139 pp. (Dissertation. University of Zurich.)   318
Deals almost exclusively with the semantic and linguistic aspects of Caxton's writings, both original and in translation. Though not directly pertinent to printing, this thorough, highly scholarly work is a considerable contribution to a fuller understanding of Caxton's importance in a cultural and literary context.

WILSON, ROBERT H.   "Caxton's Chess Book." *Modern Language Notes*, 62 (1947), 93-102.   319
Examines in detail the textual differences between the Bruges and Westminster editions of this work. Important as textual criticism.

BÜHLER, CURT F.   "Chaucer's 'House of Fame'; Another Caxton Variant." *Bibliographical Society of America. Papers*, 42 (1948), 140-143.   320
Finds the pages of one sheet of the Vienna copy were set at a different time from the same pages in the other three copies extant (Rylands, British Museum, and Cambridge). The Vienna pages have their own variants.

BÜIILER, CURT F.   "The Headlines of William de Machlinia's

Year Book, 37 Henry VI." *The Bibliographical Society of the University of Virginia. Papers*, 1 (1948-1949), 125-132.   321
  Offers possible explanations for the curious order of the headlines in this work.

BOWERS, FREDSON. "Printing Evidence in Wynkyn de Worde's Edition of 'The Life of Johan Picus' by Sir Thomas More." *Bibliographical Society of America. Publications*, 43 (1949), 398-399.   322
  A brief note on half-sheet imposition relating to this 1500(?) imprint from Wynkyn de Worde's press.

BÜHLER, CURT F. "The British Museum Fragment of Lydgate's *Horse, Sheep and Goose*, Printed by Caxton." *Bibliographical Society of America. Papers*, 43 (1949), 397-398.   323
  A brief description of the leaves and speculation as to the reasons why they might have been used for binding.

LEGMAN, G. "A Word on Caxton's *Dictes*." *The Library*, 5th ser., 3 (1949), 155-185.   324
  An attempt to refute C. F. Bühler's theory that the sequence of the two editions of the *Dictes* should be reversed (*The Library*, 4th ser., 21 [1941], entry No. 299). The author uses textual and typographical analysis to substantiate his theory. (See Bühler's reply in *The Library*, 1953, entry No. 348).

MARY JEREMY, SISTER. "Caxton's Original Additions to the *Legenda Aurea*." *Modern Language Notes*, 64 (1949), 259-261. 325
  Cites what appear to be several original additions by Caxton as translator. Also notes a number of brief insertions and variations introduced by the translator.

MUNBY, A. N. L. "Jacob Bryant's Caxtons: Some Additions to de Ricci's *Census*." *The Library*, 5th ser., 3 (1949), 218-222.   326
  Includes a sketchy biography of Jacob Bryant (1716-1804), an early Caxton authority. This is followed by a list of twelve Caxtons, whose ownership is traced. These were not listed by de Ricci (see No. 170).

SHEPPARD, L. A. "The Early Ownership of the British Museum Copy of Caxton's *Recuyell of the History of Troy*." *The Library*, 5th ser., 3 (1949), 216-218.   327
  Traces the ownership of this copy.

BENNETT, HENRY STANLEY. "Printers, Authors, and Readers, 1475-1557." *The Library*, 5th ser., 4 (1950), 155-165.   328
  A discussion of the book trade in England from Caxton to the founding of the Stationers Company. Very slight for the 15th century.

BENNETT, J. A. W. "Caxton and Gower." *Modern Language Review*, 45 (1950), 215-216.   329

A brief note indicating that Caxton used a short passage from Gower's *Confessio amantis* in his version of Ovid's *Metamorphoses*.

BINNS, A. L. "A Manuscript Source of the Book of St. Albans." *The John Rylands Library. Bulletin*, 33 (1950), 15-24.   330

Deals only with the MS version, not with the printed book.

BÜHLER, CURT F. "Observations on Two Caxton Variants [Lydgate, *Pilgrimage of the Soul*, 1483, and Christine de Pisan, *Book of the Fayttes of Armes*, 1489]." *Studies in Bibliography*, 3 (1950-1951), 97-104.   331

Evidence of two compositors (p. 99).
Caxton's use of guide letters for rubricators (pp. 99–100).
Variant use of virgule by two compositors (p. 101).
Errors in Caxton colophons (p. 103).
The presumption that Caxton had only one press (p. 104).

MORGAN, MARGERY M. "A Specimen of Early Printer's Copy, Rylands English Ms. 2." *The John Rylands Library. Bulletin*, 33 (1950-1951), 194-196.   332

The MS is a mid-15th-century copy of Lydgate's *Fall of Princes* with marginal numberings indicating that it may have been used as the copy for Pynson's 1494 edition of the work.

BENNETT, HENRY STANLEY. "Notes on English Book Prices, 1480-1560." *The Library*, 5th ser., 5 (1951), 172-178.   333

A listing of books and their prices. The books are listed by their *STC* numbers.

LETTS, MALCOLM. "The Source of the Woodcuts in Wynkyn de Worde's Edition of Mandeville's *Travels*, 1499." *The Library*, 5th ser., 6 (1951), 154-161.   334

A brief history of this immensely popular book which goes back to the 14th century. Wynkyn de Worde took a majority of the woodcuts from a German translation by Martin Welser, who printed the work in Augsburg in 1482.

"Table Showing de Worde's Woodcuts with References to Welser's Edition of 1482 and East's Edition of 1568" (pp. 157-161).

MITCHNER, R. W. "Wynkyn de Worde's Use of the Plimpton MS. of *De proprietatibus rerum*." *The Library*, 5th ser., 6 (1951), 7-18.   335

A detailed examination of the Plimpton MS (de Ricci No. 263) now at Columbia University. This MS shows printers' marks corresponding to Wynkyn de Worde's 1495 (?) edition of the work. There are indications in

the marks that several compositors set up de Worde's edition. The author
has collated the MS and the printed version and notes in tabular form the
changes made by the printer (pp. 12–17).

WILSON, ROBERT H.   "The Poggiana in Caxton's *Esope.*" *Philological Quarterly,* 30 (1951), 348–352.   336
   A brief article dealing with the sources of Caxton's Poggiana. It also
delves into the problem of Caxton's editorial omissions and alterations of
the original French text. A combination of literary history and textual criticism.

WYNNE, MARJORIE GRAY.   *"The Boke of St. Albans."* *Yale University Library Gazette,* 26 (1951), 33–36.   337
   A description of the contents of *The Boke of St. Albans* and a slight
discussion of its history on the occasion of the presentation of a 1486
copy to Yale University Library.

BENNETT, HENRY STANLEY.   *English Books and Readers, 1475–
1557. Being a Study in the History of the Book Trade from Caxton
to the Incorporation of the Stationers' Company.* Cambridge [Eng.],
1952. xiii, 336 pp.   338
   An excellent study examining the general literary, cultural, historical,
economic, and social environment of the period applied specifically to the
world of the book.
   Appendix I: "Handlist of Publications by Wynkyn de Worde" (pp. 239–
276).
   Appendix II: "Trial List of Translations into English Printed Between
1475–1560" (pp. 277–319).

BÜHLER, CURT F.   "The Morgan Copy of Machlinia's *Speculum
Christiani." Studies in Bibliography,* 5 (1952–1953), 159–160. 339
   Describes a unique variant copy of Machlinia's *Speculum Christiani.*
Supposes that the printer turned the sheet in question the wrong way, still
getting a correct register.

BÜHLER, CURT F.   "Yale's New Caxton." *Yale University Library Gazette,* 27 (1952), 12–18.   340
   Deals with the *Dictes and Sayings of the Philosophers.* The article provides an excellent brief appraisal of Caxton's activities and contributions
as well as a discussion and description of the first dated work to be printed
in England.

KINSMAN, ROBERT S.   "The Printer and Date of Publication of
Skelton's *Agaynste a Comely Coystrowne* and *Dyuers Balettys."*
Huntington Library Quarterly, 26 (1952–1953), 203–210.   341
   On the basis of internal evidence and a comparison of the two works
noted in the title with Skelton's *A Replycacion (STC* 22609), which is

known to have been printed by Pynson, the author seeks to establish the theory that the two other works were printed, not by Pynson, but by John Rastell between 1524 and 1530.

OLDHAM, JAMES BASIL. *English Blind-stamped Bindings.* Cambridge [Eng.], 1952. (The Sandars Lectures, 1949.) 342
The three lectures discuss identification, description, locale, and dating of blind-stamped panels going back to the 15th century.

PAFORT, ELOISE. "Notes on the Wynkyn de Worde Editions of the *Boke of St. Albans* and its Separates." *Studies in Bibliography,* 5 (1952-1953), 43-52. 343
A general discussion of the various editions, stressing particularly attempts at dating them. Only one, the 1492 issue, was printed in the 15th century.

REED, TALBOT BAINES. *A History of the Old English Letter Foundries; With Notes, Historical and Biographical, on the Rise and Progress of English Typography.* New ed., rev. and enl. by A. F. Johnson. London, 1952. xiv, 400 pp. 344
Revisions and expansions are very slight for the 15th century. See No. 96 for full entry.

SHEPPARD, L. A. "A New Light on Caxton and Colard Mansion." *Signature,* 15 (1952), 28-39. 345
States that Caxton taught Mansion the art of printing. Uses Wynkyn de Worde's edition of *De proprietatibus rerum* as one of his supporting arguments. Follows the theory that Caxton learned printing in Cologne. Believes that the *Recuyell* may have been printed as early as 1473. Also attributes some books to Caxton that are generally thought to have been printed by Mansion.

BINNS, NORMAN E. *An Introduction to Historical Bibliography.* London, 1953. 2nd rev. ed., London, 1962. 370 pp. 346
A general work intended for the professional student of library science. Parts of Chapter IX (pp. 111-120) deal with 15th-century printing in London, and part of Chapter X (pp. 130-134) treats 15th-century provincial printing. States that Caxton employed Wynkyn de Worde to assist in typesetting while still at Bruges and that the Bruges press was Caxton's rather than Mansion's. Does not substantiate this.

BÜHLER, CURT F. "The First Edition of *The Abbey of the Holy Ghost.*" *Studies in Bibliography,* 6, (1953-1954), 101-106. 347
The first detailed description of the only known copy of this edition of Wynkyn de Worde's *Abbey of the Holy Ghost.* Compares this edition (1496) with the copies owned by the Cambridge University Library (Duff 1) and the Folger Library (Duff 2). A detailed bibliographical and textual examination.

BÜHLER, CURT F.   "Some Observations on *The Dictes and Say-ings of the Philosophers.*"   *The Library,* 5th ser., 8 (1953), 77–88.   348
   A reasoned, rational reply to Legman's "A Word on Caxton's *Dictes*" in *The Library* (see entry No. 324). Bühler points out the contradictory state-ments in the article and seeks to develop a logical basis for at least cast-ing doubt on the generally accepted sequence of Caxton's editions.

BUTTERWORTH, CHARLES G.   "The Lord's Prayer Is Printed in London."   [University of Pennsylvania] *Library Chronicle,* 19 (1953), 93–98.   349
   Discusses an English version of the Lord's Prayer found in a little re-ligious treatise printed by Wynkyn de Worde about 1500. Includes a de-tailed description of the contents of the book as well as a fairly wide-ranging discussion of earlier English-language translations of Biblical passages.

"A Choice Decade of English Books."   *Yale University Library Gazette,* 28 (1953), 53–55.   350
   Brief description of books printed by Caxton, Wynkyn de Worde, Pynson, and Machlinia as well as by some 16th-century printers presented to Yale University Library.

JACKSON, WILLIAM A.   "Three Printed English Indulgences at Harvard."   *Harvard Library Bulletin,* 7 (1953), 229–231.   351
   Lists and describes an indulgence printed by Julian Notary in 1503, is-sued under authority of Alexander VI. This is the only known copy.
   The second indulgence, in two settings, was probably printed by Pynson between 1511 and 1518.
   The third, printer again uncertain, may have been printed by Wynkyn de Worde about 1520.

MORGAN, MARGERY M.   "Pynson's Manuscript of *Dives and Pau-per.*"   *The Library,* 5th ser., 8 (1953), 217–228.   352
   A detailed description and discussion of the MS now in the Bodleian Li-brary. The author assumes that it is the one used by Pynson for his print-ing.

MORTIMER, JEAN E.   "An Unrecorded Caxton at Ripon Cathe-dral."   *The Library,* 5th ser., 8 (1953), 37–42.   353
   The work is Laurentius Gulielmus of Savona's *Epitome Margaritae eloquentiae* (1480?). The article provides a description and brief history of this copy together with a general discussion of its cultural importance.

RUYSSCHAERT, JOSÉ.   "Les manuscrits autographes de deux oeuvres de Lorenzo Guglielmo Traversagni imprimées chez Cax-

ton.'' *The John Rylands Library. Bulletin,* 36 (1953-1954), 191–
197. 354
An examination of two MS copies leads the author to theorize that Caxton had a text different from the Vatican MS (Vat. lat. 11441). Traversagni
probably made a copy of his work while in England and Caxton printed
from that.

WINGER, HOWARD W. ''Regulations Relating to the Booktrade in
London from 1357 to 1586.'' (Unpublished thesis, University of Il-
linois, 1953.) 355
Not examined. See article by Winger (No. 368).

BÜHLER, CURT F. ''Corrections in Caxton's *Cordiale* (1497).''
Bibliographical Society of America. Papers, 48 (1954),
194-196. 356
A discussion and description of the stop-press corrections in this work
based on examination of 12 copies.

MARSTEN, THOMAS E. ''The First Illustrated Edition of the *Canterbury Tales.*'' *Yale University Library Gazette,* 28 (1954), 150–
152. 357
A description of a copy of Caxton's 1484(?) printing which was presented to Yale.

MEAD, HERMAN R. ''A New Title from de Worde's Press.'' *The
Library,* 5th ser., 9 (1954), 45–49. 358
Describes the only recorded copy of *Octavian*. This was formerly as-
cribed to the press of Copland but is here attributed to that of Wynkyn de
Worde about 1504–1506.

BENNETT, HENRY STANLEY. ''Notes on Two Incunables: *The
Abbey of the Holy Ghost* and *A Ryght Profytable Treatyse.*'' *The
Library,* 5th ser., 10 (1955), 120–121. 359
Points out that Wynkyn de Worde's printing of *The Abbey* is actually two
works in that the latter is sandwiched between parts of *The Charter of the
Abbey of the Holy Ghost.*
Establishes the spelling of the name of the compiler of *A Ryght Profyt-
able Treatyse* as Betson.

KERLING, NELLY J. M. ''Caxton and the Trade in Printed
Books.'' *The Book Collector,* 4 (1955), 190-199. 360
The author searched all the extant accounts of the Port of London for
material for this article. She presents here, for the first time, clear evidence that Caxton not only printed and sold the products of his press but
also engaged in importing books. The earliest evidence for this is dated
Feb. 25, 1488. Caxton may have begun importing earlier; records immediately preceding this period have not been preserved. The same year (1488)

there is also a record that Caxton exported 140 volumes, title not mentioned. Nothing has been found to indicate any further activity of this sort after 1488.

MITCHELL, WILLIAM SMITH. *A History of Scottish Bookbinding, 1432-1650.* Edinburgh, London, 1955. (Aberdeen University Studies, No. 134.)   361
    I. "The Fifteenth Century" (pp. 1–10).
    II. "The Fifteenth to Early Sixteenth Century" (pp. 11–26).
    This study is the outgrowth of a doctoral thesis of 1955. Examines not only Scottish binding but also compares it with European binding in general. Includes discussions and descriptions of bindings.
    Appendix A: "Scottish Bookbinders Before 1650" (pp. 118–128).
    Plates 1–4 are of 15th-century bindings.

AVIS, F. C. "English Printers' Marks of the Incunabula Period." *Gutenberg Jahrbuch* (1956), pp. 111–115.   362
    An illustrated discussion and description of 15th-century printers' marks.

BÜHLER, CURT F. "The Newberry Library Manuscript of the *Dictes and Sayings of the Philosophers.*" *Anglia,* 74 (1956), 281–291.   363
    A comparison of the MS with the two printed Caxton texts.

FORMAN, P. "Two Rare Books in the University Library, Glasgow." *The Bibliotheck,* 1 (1956), 22–23.   364
    The volume pertinent here is a possibly unique copy of Sulpicius' *Grammer* printed by Wynkyn de Worde between 1506 and 1518. The other work is Scott's *Mensa philosophica* (1609).

RHODES, D. E. "Variants in the 1479 Oxford Edition of Aristotle's *Ethics.*" *Studies in Bibliography,* 8, (1956), 209–212. . 365
    Examines all eight known copies of the work for variants in reset forme and for press variants. Concludes that the book was printed in formes of only two pages. The copies examined are: British Museum, C.2.a.7; British Museum, Grenville 7930; Bodleian Library, Seld.e.2; All Souls College, L.R.4.e.14; Chetham's Library (Manchester); John Rylands Library, No. 15969; Chapin Library, and Broxbourne Library.

ROGERS, D. M. "The 'Friends of North Newington'; A New Pynson Broadside." *Bodleian Library Record,* 5 (1956), 251–255.   366
    Pynson here used a copy of a woodcut previously used by Wynkyn de Worde in his printing of the *Golden Legend.* The broadside was printed in 1521. The article discusses its content and printing history.

WELCH, C. E. "Julian Notary and Andrew Rowe: Two Contemporary Records." *The Library,* 5th ser., 11 (1956), 277–278.   367

A brief note on two entries found in the records of the Bishop of London. The one dealing with Notary seems to establish clearly that he was a native of Vannes in Brittany.

WINGER, HOWARD W. "Regulations Relating to the Book Trade in London from 1357 to 1586." *The Library Quarterly,* 26 (1956), 157–195.   368
Of primary pertinence is the section titled "The Growth of Printing, 1477–1519" (pp. 163–165).
The author points out that none of the early printers were members of the Stationers' Company. Initially the Crown protected and patronized the new art, but there was little direct regulation in the period before 1501.

BAKER, C. M. "Bookbinding and Bookbinders in London, 1403–1603; a Survey of Their Legal, Economic, and Social Status." (Unpublished thesis, University of Chicago, 1957.)   369
Not examined.

LEACH, MACEDWARD, ed. *Paris and Vienne. Translated from the French and Printed by William Caxton.* London, New York, 1957. xxxi, 120 pp. (Early English Text Society, No. 234.)   370
"The Different Versions of the Story" (pp. ix–xvi). Discusses and compares the different manuscript and printed versions. Describes the Caxton text (pp. xi–xii). Cites and compares passages of the two basically different versions.
"The Origin and the Date of the Story" (pp. xvi–xxii).
"Caxton and the Story in French" (pp. xxii–xxvi). Points out that the Caxton version is very close to the one printed by Leeu and to a French MS (B. N. Fr. 20044).
"Caxton as a Translator" (xxvi–xxxi). The editor considers the Caxton translation a good one in spite of some minor defects. Emphasizes that Caxton's skill in translation increased considerably after a dubious beginning. Examines the syntax and style and also the textual changes and additions made by Caxton.

MORGAN, PAUL. "A Caxton Discovery at Warwick." *Times Literary Supplement* (Jan. 18, 1957), p. 40.   371
Legenda festivitatum... Paris, by Guillaume Maynyal for Caxton, 1488 (de Ricci 101, Duff 247, *STC* 16136, GW 5447).
The article briefly describes a more complete copy discovered at the Collegiate Church of St. Mary, Warwick.

MORGAN, PAUL and PAINTER, G. D. "The Caxton *Legenda* at St. Mary's, Warwick." *The Library,* 5th ser., 12 (1957), 225–239.   372
A detailed and thorough study and analysis.
1. "The Library of St. Mary's, Warwick, and the Discovery of the Caxton *Legenda*" (pp. 225–227).

2. "Bibliographical Description of the Caxton *Legenda*" (pp. 227–230).

3. "Caxton and Guillaume Maynyal. The Printing and Publishing of the *Legenda*" (pp. 230–234).

4. "The Text of the Caxton *Legenda*" (pp. 234–236).

5. "The Condition and Provenance of the Caxton *Legenda*" (pp. 236–239).

SHORTER, ALFRED H.   *Paper Mills and Paper Makers in England, 1495–1800.* Vol. VI of *Monumenta chartae papyraceae historiam illustrantia.* Hilversum [Holland], 1957. 457 pp.   373
   Only slight references to the 15th century.
   John Tate's will, p. 27.
   Map of "Paper Mills in England, 1495–1600" (p. 92).
   Appendix C: "List of Watermarks" (p. 259). Lists three 15th-century marks illustrated on p. 271.

SIMKO, JÁN.   *Word-Order in the Winchester Manuscript and in William Caxton's Edition of Thomas Malory's "Morte Darthur" (1485)—A Comparison.* Halle [Germany], 1957. xii, 122 pp.   374
   A study of syntax and word-order variations. By regularizing variations Caxton helped establish many of the basic patterns of contemporary English usage.
   An extremely detailed analysis by a Czech scholar; of considerable value to the philologist, grammarian, and literary scholar.

TANNER, LAWRENCE E.   "William Caxton's Houses at Westminster." *The Library,* 5th ser., 12 (1957), 153–166.   375
   A detailed history of the houses owned and used by Caxton. Much of this work is based on examination of various contemporary records.

BOON, K. G.   "Was Colard Mansion de illustrator van 'Le Livre de la Ruyne des Nobles Hommes et Femmes'?" *Amor Librorum. Bibliographic and Other Essays; a Tribute to Abraham Horodisch on His Sixtieth Birthday.* Zurich, Amsterdam, 1958. pp. 85–88.   376
   The work discussed here, a translation of Boccaccio's *De casibus illustrium virorum illustrium,* was printed by Mansion in 1476 in Bruges. The author concludes that Mansion did not illustrate it himself.

COLEMAN, DONALD C.   *The British Paper Industry, 1495–1860.* Oxford, 1958. xvi, 367 pp.   377
   Only the briefest references to the incunabula period. The work is a general history of the paper industry stressing the economic aspects.

JENNETT, SEÁN.   "William Caxton, the Introduction of Printing into England," *Pioneers in Printing.* London, 1958. pp. 28–46. 378
   With no indication of sources or explanation, the author flatly states that Caxton learned his art at Cologne and subsequently instructed Mansion in

it. Delves somewhat into printing techniques. Downgrades Caxton's technical achievements and does not evaluate Caxton's literary and linguistic contribution.

OATES, J. C. T. "Richard Pynson and the *Holy Blood of Hayles.*" *The Library*, 5th ser., 13 (1958), 269–277. 379

The article discusses the only known copy of a work printed by Pynson (c. 1515) dealing with the miracles attributed to the relic at the Cistercian Abbey of Hayles.

OLDHAM, JAMES BASIL. *Blind Panels of English Binders.* Cambridge [Eng.], 1958. xv, 55 pp. 380

Companion volume to the same author's *English Blind-stamped Bindings* (No. 342). Panels are grouped according to subjects. Contains general discussion and detailed descriptions of panels. Plates are rubbings of panels.

RHODES, D. E. *"The Remorse of Conscience."* The Library, 5th ser., 13 (1958), 199–200. 381

Examines and dates three editions of Wynkyn de Worde's printing of the *Remorse of Conscience.* Two are listed in the *STC* (20882, 20883) with "1500?" given for both. The third is a fragment at Sion College.

HARNETT, CYNTHIA. *Caxton's Challenge.* Cleveland, New York, [1959, 1960]. 254 pp. Published in England under the title *The Load of Unicorn.* 382

An illustrated novel with Caxton as central figure. Intended for youngsters. Charmingly written and as far as Caxton is concerned essentially accurate as to specific details, though the conversations and some characters are obviously invented.

MORGAN, PAUL. *English Provincial Printing.* [n.p.], 1959. 18 pp. 383

A lecture delivered at the School of Librarianship, College of Commerce, Birmingham. Contains only brief reference to 15th-century printing (p. 4).

STEINBERG, SIGFRID HENRY. *Five Hundred Years of Printing.* New York, [1959]. 384

A concise general history of printing. England for the incunabula period and early 16th century, pp. 72–79.

BÜHLER, CURT F. *William Caxton and His Critics.* Syracuse, 1960. vii, 30 pp. (Brewster House Typographical Series, No. 3.) 385

A brief essay evaluating Caxton's contribution to the English language and to English letters. The little work places Caxton in perspective with respect to his great contribution as a taste setter.

Includes Caxton's prologue to *Eneydos* in facsimile together with a modern English version.

HANDOVER, P. M.   *Printing in London from 1476 to Modern Times: Competitive Practice and Technical Invention in the Trade of Book and Bible Printing, Periodical Production, Jobbing, etc.* London, Cambridge [Mass.], 1960. 224 pp.   386
    Only the briefest coverage of 15th-century printing (pp. 22–23). The slight material pertaining to the 15th century hardly justifies the title of the book, much less the title imprinted on the dust jacket, "Printing in London from Caxton to Modern Times." The work is useful as an account of English publishing monopolies, but since these started in the 16th century, there is little here of value to the incunabulist.

MORAN, JAMES.   *Wynkyn de Worde, Father of Fleet Street.* London, 1960. 55 pp.   387
    A general biography of Wynkyn de Worde, based primarily on the research done by earlier scholars, particularly Plomer. Presents a balanced evaluation of de Worde, establishing that he was essentially a craftsman and tradesman and was less cognizant of the cultural and literary values of his product than was his one-time employer, Caxton. The author claims that by providing what the public wanted de Worde "was also the forerunner of the popular press lords and hence the father of Fleet Street in its wider sense."

RHODES, D. E.   "Some Documents Printed by Pynson for St. Botolph's, Boston, Lincs." *The Library*, 5th ser., 15 (1960), 53–57.
                                                                        388
    Describes and discusses eight documents printed by Pynson in the 16th century, including those listed in numbers 17549–17551 in the *STC*.

RHODES, D. E.   "Two Issues of an Indulgence of Alexander VI." *The Library*, 5th ser., 15 (1960), 206–207.   389
    Describes and discusses two indulgences printed by Wynkyn de Worde, probably between 1503 and 1506. Neither is listed in the *STC*.

SANDS, DONALD B., ed.   *The History of Reynard the Fox. Translated and Printed by William Caxton in 1481.* Cambridge [Mass.], 1960. viii, 224 pp.   390
    The editor states (p. 10) that Caxton used the Middle Dutch Gouda text for his translation, although earlier scholars were at least doubtful or uncertain (see Duff, *The Cambridge History of English Literature*, entry No. 165).
    Chapter II, "William Caxton's Discovery of Reynard the Fox," presents a general, brief, biographical sketch together with an evaluation of Caxton, specifically relating him to this work.

STUART, DOROTHY MARGARET.   "William Caxton: Mercer,

Translator and Master Printer." *History Today,* 10 (1960), 256–264. 391

A brief, general biography of no particular originality or value.

LENAGHAN, R. T. "The Variants in Caxton's 'Esope.'" *Bibliographical Society of America. Publications,* 55 (1961), 34–36. 392

A brief listing and examination of the variants in three copies of *Esope* (British Museum, Royal Library at Windsor, and the Bodleian Library).

MORAN, JAMES. "William Blades." *The Library,* 5th ser., 16 (1961), 251–266. (Read before the Bibliographical Society on 21 March 1961). 393

Gives a brief history of the printing firm of which Blades was a partner as well as a professional and personal biography of Blades. Also points out a number of errors and erroneous assumptions made by Blades in his research on type identification, his theory of line endings, and particularly his absolute rejection of the idea that Caxton learned printing at Cologne. The author feels that Blades occasionally tailored the evidence to suit his theories, especially in his rejection of Wynkyn de Worde's prohemium to the *De proprietatibus rerum.* Agrees with Duff, however, in his evaluation of Blades's immense contribution to bibliography.

OLDHAM, J. B. "English Fifteenth Century Binding," *Festschrift Ernst Kyriss.* Stuttgart, 1961. pp. 159–174. 394

Points out (p. 164) that Caxton, Pynson, and Rood and Hunt possibly kept binderies of their own and that Pynson may have been a binder himself.

Discusses and describes individual bindings and their characteristic designs.

HANFORD, J. H. "'De proprietatibus rerum' of Bartholomaeus Anglicus." *Princeton University Library Chronicle,* 23 (1962), 126–130. 395

Written on the acquisition by Princeton of a copy of the Wynkyn de Worde printing of c. 1495. Gives the literary and printing history of the book which contains the poem stating that Caxton had printed a Latin version of the work at Cologne.

WILLIAMS, MELVIN G. "Caxton and Literary Taste." *Black Art,* 1 (1962), 119–121. 396

A brief summarization of the frequently opposing views regarding Caxton's literary taste and his contribution to English letters. Contrasts primarily Duff's essay in the *Cambridge History of English Literature* (No. 105) and H. S. Bennett's *English Books and Readers* (No. 338). Williams does not think Caxton was a conscious reformer, but rather a popularizer with taste and ability. Does not discuss Caxton's contribution as a printer.

BREKLE, HERBERT ERNST. *Semantische Analyse von Wertad-
jektiven als Determinanten persönlicher Substantive in William Caxtons Prologen und Epilogen.* [Tübingen, 1963.] (Dissertation, University of Tübingen.)   397
   Not examined.

HELLINGA, LOTTE and HELLINGA, WYTZE GS. *Colard Man-
sion; An Original Leaf from the "Ovide moralizé," Bruges, 1484.*
Amsterdam, 1963. 15 pp.   398
   Not examined. Only 40 copies of this edition were printed.

MUSCATINE, CHARLES. *The Book of Geoffrey Chaucer. An Account of the Publication of Geoffrey Chaucer's Works from the Fifteenth Century to Modern Times.* [San Francisco], 1963. 64 pp.
   Not examined.   399

PAINTER, GEORGE D. "Caxton Through the Looking-Glass. An
Enquiry into the Offsets on a Fragment of Caxton's Fifteen Oes.
With a Census of Caxton Bindings." *Gutenberg Jahrbuch* (1963),
pp. 73–80.   400
   Discusses in detail the offsets on a fragment of the *Fifteen Oes* ex-
amined earlier by Henry Bradshaw in 1877 (see No. 76).
   Finds that the offsets are from "otherwise unknown editions of the
Sarum *Horae,* printed with material common to both Caxton and Wynkyn de
Worde, and that the circumstantial evidence seems in favour of Caxton as
printer, though certainty is not possible" (p. 80).

BLAKE, N. F. "William Caxton's *Reynard the Fox* and His Dutch
Original." *The John Rylands Library. Bulletin,* 46 (1964), 298–
325.   401
   In Part I the author tries to establish the Dutch source for Caxton's
translation. Part II is a comparison of the Dutch original with Caxton's
version. The author compares specific passages from a linguistic and sty-
listic viewpoint.

OATES, J. C. T. and HARMER, L. C., eds. *Vocabulary in French
and English. A Facsimile of Caxton's Edition c. 1480.* Cambridge
[Eng.], 1964. xxxvi, 49 pp.   402
   A photo-reprint of the *Dialogues in French and English* (see also Bradley, No. 133).
   "Textual Introduction," by L. C. Harmer (pp. ix–xxxi).
   A fairly detailed examination of the textual history of the work. Also
discusses the linguistic, orthographic, and morphological aspects. Finds
numerous grammatical errors in Caxton's French text as well as an exces-
sive number of misspellings and a frequently too literal translation.
   "Bibliographical Introduction" (by J. C. T. Oates) (pp. xxxiii–[xxxvi]).

This facsimile is of No. 97 (1) in de Ricci's *Census*. It is printed in Caxton's type 4 without signatures. The author describes and compares the copy here reproduced with the three other extant ones (John Rylands Library, Durham University Library, and Huntington Library). Because of the many typographical errors in the French text and as the result of comparing these errors with the lower incidence of accidentals in the English text, Oates believes that Caxton's compositor "knew little, if any, French."

Index

The index lists, alphabetically, the major topics, titles, printers, authors, editors, and compilers. Figures following the headings and subheadings refer to entry numbers, not pages.

A

B

D

E

F

G

H

I

L

M

N

O

Printing:

  England:

    15th century,   32–41, 43, 47–48, 79, 82, 165, 222, 224
       346

    and/or later periods,   79–80, 83, 96, 110, 135, 187, 203,
       215–217, 344, 386

    economic history,   132, 153, 157, 160, 172, 201, 212, 236, 239,
       282, 287, 328, 333, 338, 355, 360, 368

    general histories,   32, 34–35, 47, 110, 188, 214–215, 222, 297,
       302, 307, 345–346, 384

    see also Typography

Prior, O. H., *Caxton's "Mirrour of the World,"*   185

Proctor, Robert, *An Index to the Early Printed Books in the British Museum*,   3

Prologues and epilogues, *see* Caxton, William

Propositio Johannis Russell,   171

Provincial printers,   123, 176, 383

  see also Oxford, printing at; St. Albans, printing at

Public records,   196, 201, 220, 360, 367, 375

Pylgremage of the Sowle,   246, 331

Pynson Richard,   39, 76, 95, 117, 128, 132, 139, 143–146, 157,
    161, 163, 172, 182, 196, 203, 251, 263, 332, 352

  facsimiles,   124, 126, 183, 218, 264

  imprints,   189, 198, 252, 258, 279–280, 316, 350–351, 366, 379,
    388

  typography,   124, 126, 150, 218, 279, 306, 341

Q

Quantin, Albert, *Les origines de l'imprimerie ... en Angleterre*,   82

Quatre fils Aimon, see *Four Sons of Aimon*

R

Rae, John, *The Statutes of Henry VII ... Printed by Caxton*,   65

Ramage, David, *A Finding-List of English Books to 1640*,   28

Rastell, John (printer),   341

Recuyell of the Historyes of Troy,   121, 243, 257, 269, 327

Redgrave, G. R., *see* Pollard, A. W.,   15

Reed, T. B.:

  A History of the Old English Letter Foundries,   96, 344

  see Blades, William,   110

Reference books, *see* Bibliographies; Catalogs; Checklists; Indexes

S

T

W

Y